THE STUDY OF MODERN MANUSCRIPTS

THE JAMES P. R. LYELL LECTURES
IN BIBLIOGRAPHY FOR 1989

THE
STUDY
OF MODERN
MANUSCRIPTS

PUBLIC, CONFIDENTIAL,
AND PRIVATE

DONALD H. REIMAN

❖

THE
JOHNS HOPKINS
UNIVERSITY PRESS
BALTIMORE AND
LONDON

This book has been brought to publication with the generous assistance of the James P. R. Lyell Fund, Oxford University.

The Johns Hopkins University Press
2715 North Charles Street
Baltimore, Maryland 21218-4319
The Johns Hopkins Press Ltd., London

Library of Congress Cataloging-in-Publication Data
Reiman, Donald H.
The study of modern manuscripts : public, confidential, and private /
Donald H. Reiman.
p.   cm.
"James P. R. Lyell lectures in bibliography for 1989."
Includes bibliographical references (p.   ) and index.
ISBN 0-8018-4590-4 (acid-free paper)
1. English literature—19th century—Criticism, Textual.   2. Literature,
Modern—Criticism, Textual.   3. Manuscripts, English—Editing.
4. Manuscripts—Editing.   I. Title.
PR468.T48R45   1993
801'.959—dc20   92-43641

8695969

For Jack Stillinger

" . . . so you see I am inclined enough to take
your advice now. I must express once more
my deep sense of your kindness . . . ."

—KEATS TO SHELLEY

CONTENTS

❖

PREFACE

❖

Although the thesis and examples in this volume were first
tested in May 1989 by the reactions of the bibliographical
specialists from Oxford and London who regularly attend the
James P. R. Lyell Lectures in Bibliography, they are as much
concerned with English poetry, the theory and practice of
editing literary texts, and the theory of literary criticism as
they are with the history of the production, classification, and
bibliographical description of modern manuscripts as artifacts.
My envisioned readers include both curators of rare books
and manuscripts and teachers and students of English and
American literature, especially those whose interests center on
the last two hundred years and those who have been involved
in the interwoven debates on issues of literary and textual
theory. Since the founding of the Society for Textual Scholarship (STS) and the inauguration of its annual publication
TEXT: Transactions of the Society for Textual Scholarship,
the theoretical discussions of issues originating in descriptive
and analytical bibliography, paleography, codicology, and
other disciplines traditionally thought of by students of post-
Renaissance literature as nonliterary, technical specializations
have been shown to have direct literary implications for later
periods, as well as for the studies of classicists and medievalists.

    D. C. Greetham has argued in the preface to his ground-
breaking new handbook, *Textual Scholarship: An Introduction,* that since the advent of STS and *TEXT,* bibliographical
"processes, even the most technical, can also be seen as aspects
of the 'textuality' of textual scholarship, the problematization
and conceptionalization of the ontology of the text, work,

edition, and the consequent re-examination of the status of author, scribe, compositor, redactor, and editor."[1] In other words, the mode of theoretical questioning by poststructuralist critics and theorists that has for the past two decades examined the status and meaning of texts in literary studies has now seeped into the foundations of literary studies to interrogate the status and efficacy of the basic techniques by which texts are first established, before they reach the hands of most readers, teachers, students, and critics. This pursuit of fundamental questions to the source of potential problems thus deserves etymologically the appellation "a *radical* re-examination," whatever may be the political implications of its various incarnations.

Having been active in STS since the planning for its first international conference and having participated in all of the succeeding conferences to date, I have watched this evolution firsthand and have even played a modest part in the debates initiated within the ranks of the editors and bibliographers who have regularly attended its biennial conferences or contributed to *TEXT*. As will be seen, my concern has been to be sure that the baby not be thrown out with the bath water — to add common sense to the mix so that our advances in sophisticated analysis of the tenuous grasp that human beings have upon all ontological realities and evaluative meanings do not degenerate into sophistic arguments leading to a radical relativism or textual nihilism that would permit universal problematics to cover all. As a student of the historical Skeptical tradition from Pyrrho of Elis to David Hume and Sir William Drummond, I am not unsympathetic to the probing of unexamined assumptions, but I also remember that the self-appointed task of the greatest of those Skeptical philosophers — Cicero, Montaigne, and Hume — was to defeat the attempts of new intellectual dogmatisms, backed by political power, to impose arbitrary standards of political, religious, or rational correctness on the societies in which these thinkers lived.

This much forewarning should help reorient readers who may pick up the book under the false surmise that it is a technical manual on how to date or describe manuscripts of the modern era. It is, rather, a mildly theoretical study that defines and describes different categories of modern manuscripts based on the functions their authors intended them to play in communicating with specific intended readers. The volume is bolstered by numerous specific examples that (in the manner of Hume's) are designed both to illustrate my definitions and generalizations and to test their limits and their practical applications. Many of these examples are drawn from my thirty-odd years of experience in working with the manuscripts of the Shelleys, Byron, and their circles, and some of the ideas expressed here have developed from the more narrowly focused papers on textual and literary criticism represented in my *Romantic Texts and Contexts* (1987). But in the present volume, even specialists in the English Romantics will find novelties among the instances drawn from this field, and I have also included other examples and questions relating to a variety of other periods and disciplines to tease students of several disciplines into thinking about implications of bibliographical and textual analysis for their own studies.

·

A central concern of these lectures was the distinctions between *personal* (or "private"), *confidential* (or "corporate"), and *public* manuscripts—distinctions of which few scholars and critics seemed cognizant at the time I began discussing them. These differences have important but largely unrecognized implications for library curators who collect manuscripts; for bibliographers who classify and analyze them; for editors and critics who use them as evidence in producing texts or analyzing and explicating them; and for theorists who generalize about the nature of literary texts. As I argue, these distinctions have their origins, not in the arbitrary taxonomies of theorists, but in the distinctive intentions of the creators of the documents, literary or historical, that we inevitably encounter. Thus the focus shifts back to the relevance of authorial intentions and the vagaries of human nature.

If I have also humanized the study of modern manuscripts

by citing personal experiences and characterizing individuals involved in the anecdotes rather more than some students of bibliography might do, let readers of the final chapter testify that this personal emphasis is not unintentional. I have long been convinced that until literary teacher-scholars recognize that their studies, including the bibliographical and textual components, are recognized as operating, not at the level of scientific generalization, but at that of individual and personal experience—until, that is, they stop pretending that the study of literature is a social or physical science and recognize it as a humanistic endeavor—there will be continued distortions of the understanding of literary works and artifacts and a tendency to reduce literary studies to bloodless inanities. This book may be said, in fact, to point toward a bibliography of human interactions, marking out some of the limitations and pitfalls that await anyone who attempts to turn into a *science* the *art* of analyzing the manuscripts that provide primary evidence for understanding such intentions.

•

Without implicating in my polemical positions the friends and advisers who have been kind enough to discuss—or debate—problems with me, help me strengthen my arguments, supply information, suggest illustrative examples, or advise tacks that I might take in treating the subject, I here record my thanks to Richard De Gennaro and Rodney G. Dennis of the Harvard University Libraries; Mihai H. Handrea and Robert Sink of The New York Public Library; David G. Vaisey, R. Julian Roberts, and especially B. C. Barker-Benfield of the Bodleian Library, Oxford; Jon Stallworthy of Wolfson College, Oxford; and David C. Greetham, W. Speed Hill, and G. Thomas Tanselle of the biblio-textual brain trust in New York. For help with my search for poems-as-living-children, I thank William Keach of Brown University and Christina Shuttleworth Kraus of the Department of Classics, New York University. For more sustained counsel and for reading all or large portions of the lectures—some more than once—I thank Neil Fraistat, Doucet

Devin Fischer, Jack Stillinger, W. Speed Hill, and especially Hélène Dworzan (Reiman).

The dedication of this book to Jack Stillinger recognizes one of my longest and most helpful associations. Jack arrived to teach at Illinois in 1958, just as I was beginning to research and write my dissertation on Shelley's "The Triumph of Life." He soon became my confidant and second mentor (after Royal A. Gettmann), in which role he kindly read—and sharply and usefully critiqued—most of my writings on the Romantics during my first decade in the profession. I'm happy to admit that many of his ideas on editorial and textual theory that I resisted in our early discussions now seem self-evident to me. Today, in our give and take as collegial friends, I still enjoy his self-deprecating humor and admire the exceptional strength of his common sense—qualities that are not as frequently in evidence in the halls of academe as they once seemed to be.

THE STUDY OF MODERN MANUSCRIPTS

CHAPTER ONE

INTRODUCTION:

MODERN MANUSCRIPTS

❖

I.

By the word *manuscripts* I refer to handwritten memoranda or communications on paper and other flexible surfaces of animal or vegetable matter (such as parchment and linen) that have been used to *transmit* written records across distances — but not on stone, bronze, or materials traditionally used to *record* written messages at particular spots.[1] The phrase *"modern* manuscripts" designates those manuscripts that originated within the era since typography and the printing process joined handwriting as a primary means of conveying such records and communications. In Western civilization, this era came into flower sometime late in the fifteenth century when printers, who had hitherto disseminated primarily religious and classical texts, schoolbooks, and popular ephemeral publications, started to capture the imaginations of contemporary humanist authors who wrote for posterity, so that these authors began to send their writings to the printshop rather than to the scrivener.

Two hundred years from now, historians or theorists of texts may well decide that the age of modern manuscripts continued to the end of the twentieth century, but we already know that a new era has begun to emerge in which both casual messages and many more permanent records are being prepared primarily for electronic transmission, storage, and retrieval and only secondarily for impression on paper or kindred substances. Though we cannot be sure how posterity will judge present events and trends, the era of modern manuscripts covers at least five centuries, from about 1475 to 1975, with the beginning and ending dates marking the approximate time that technological changes alerted the forward-looking intellectuals of the transitional eras to the new modes of transmitting and recording visual data that would ultimately alter the shape of their intellectual world.

These five centuries of the era of modern manuscripts can be divided into three subdivisions—the Renaissance, the Enlightenment, and the Romantic Period. These historical divisions recognize not only differences in the intellectual spirit and activity but also the more fundamental social, economic, and ideological changes that they embodied. For purposes of treating English authors, these subdivisions can be given approximate dates. The English Renaissance took hold in the fourth decade of the sixteenth century, when the final schism between the English and Roman churches curtailed the conservative, medieval influences within England. And for practical purposes, the Renaissance ended in 1649, when the execution of Charles the First marked a major triumph of bourgeois social forces over the ideal of feudal authoritarianism—the "divine right of kings"—that had emerged during the Middle Ages but reached its apogee in Britain under the Tudor and early Stuart monarchs, after the elimination of the checks and balances on the monarchy formerly provided by the Roman Catholic church.

In the following period, which I designate the Enlightenment, the obedience to divinely constituted authority that had been implicit in the hierarchical ideal so rudely contravened by the regicides gave way to new bases for validating human societies. In the political sphere, the example of the Commonwealth, the Restoration, and the Glorious Revolution (and, in America, the success of such political experiments as the Mayflower Compact) stimulated—for instance, in the thinking of Thomas Hobbes and John Locke—ideological justifications of the very bourgeois theory of government by social contract. The political theories of Hobbes and Locke, which are conventionally depicted as contrary schools, both actually presupposed a utilitarian order in which rational individuals acquiesce to a social plan, either concurring with a beneficent natural law (Locke) or reacting against a barbaric and dangerous state of nature (Hobbes). Enlightenment thinkers viewed God as a step removed from the sublunar scheme of things, and they believed that human beings needed to use their powers of reason to maintain or improve their status in the universe. There is no need to rehearse here the history of the growth of science, the impact of Copernicus, Galileo, Descartes, and Newton, the example of the Royal Society, and so forth. The Enlightenment era clearly marked a change in the view of man's place in the universe. Just as clearly, the idea that men rationally created or accepted a social compact is a substantial distance from the older idea that human needs could be satisfied only by obeying God's anointed clerical and temporal authorities. The Enlightenment ideal promoted the study of the laws of Nature and rewarded those who advanced the sciences—particularly mathematics, physics, physiology, and economics—that spearheaded intellectual progress in the latter part of the seventeenth and most of the eighteenth century.

The Romantic era developed as an outgrowth of the Industrial Revolution, following the failure of the attempt to introduce a radical Enlightenment polity into France after 1789. Government by rational social contract, which was supposed to have resulted from the Tennis Court Oath, degenerated first into a Reign of Terror and then, after an imperial bloodbath for all Europe, into a restored shadow of the *ancien régime*. Again, we need not analyze in detail all the effects resulting from the successive changes in the goals sought by such enlightened aristocrats as La Fayette and by the bourgeois Girondin, Jacobin, and Thermidorian leaders (who pushed France toward the limits of rational regimentation) or even by Napoleon (who was content to use the leverage of mere human frailties). Recent studies of the effects of these upheavals on English literature include well-known analyses of the transition from a variety of ideological perspectives by Northrop Frye, Morse Peckham, M. H. Abrams, Marilyn Butler, and an excellent overview of the writing and graphic arts of the period, with good reproductions of many paintings and manuscripts, by Jonathan Wordsworth and his colleagues.[2] (I venture also to mention my study entitled *Intervals of Inspiration*.)[3]

From these and collateral studies there has emerged the following consensus among Romanticists: Whereas in the medieval period the tests for the truth about the nature and destiny of Man had rested on dogma and temporal authority, during the Renaissance, faith in dogma changed into a veneration of ancient and universally accepted ideas. During the Enlightenment this dependence upon intellectual and social authorities of the past gave way to a belief that the thinking and educated individual could, through the exercise of Reason, discover and recognize Truth, which would always vanquish error in the courts of rational discourse and informed public opinion. In the Romantic age (which I believe includes us in its train), a recognition of darker emotions and more basic pre(ter)-rational forces in our psyches forced the Romantics to fall back on traditional moral values and primal sentiments, the authority of which they derived not from hierarchical recommendation but from personal experience.

Later in the nineteenth century, the course taken by scientific thinking itself in the work of Darwin, Marx, and Freud led their disciples to doubt that reason could ever motivate people of diverse backgrounds and experience to agree on first principles, or, in fact, to acknowledge that there were such fundamental truths. The implications of belief in such a deeper, fundamentally irrational nature of humanity appears in the philosophical reorientation proposed by followers of Kierkegaard, Nietzsche, and Wittgenstein. In the most recent turn of events, Jacques Derrida and his followers, harping on themes that fascinated Coleridge, Shelley, and other Romantics, have raised serious questions about the capacity of language itself to communicate the experiences of one individual to others because of the limitations inherent in the arbitrary nature of all forms of discourse, which impose themselves between writer and reader and constantly either veil or unravel the sense that the writer hopes to transmit.

These changes in the intellectual climate have affected the study of manuscripts as well as literary texts during the past five centuries. Briefly (for this subject is worth a series of lectures in its own right), the philosophical reorientations that I have just outlined, together with social and technological developments that accompanied them, changed the nature and use of manuscripts at least once during each of the three ideological periods that have held sway since the invention of printing. And the changes in the uses of manuscripts have been followed by changes in both the nature of the manuscripts that survive and in the frequency of their survival.

II.

For authors during both the Middle Ages and the Renaissance, the primary texts were those of classical and early Christian authorities that conveyed the record nearest to the actual words of the primary authorities—the lectures of Aristotle, the sayings of Jesus, the pastoral letters and scriptural commentaries of the church fathers. But having the assurance that God was protecting the transmission of His truth through the direct intervention of the Holy Spirit, many of those who were responsible for copying and disseminating these texts apparently felt justified in discarding older manuscripts after they had been recopied. (At least this is one possible reason for the breaks in the survival of exemplars in various lines of transmission of classical and biblical texts.) In any case, it seems quite clear that the preservation of very old manuscripts was not a high priority during the so-called Dark Ages, when the texts on parchment codexes containing secular classical texts were often erased by scraping and the leaves reused to copy religious works of more recent date, many now considered to have less value, such as the copy of St. Augustine's commentary on the Psalms that covered the only known text of Cicero's *De re publica*.[4] But the principle remained that those copying texts attempted (within their individual capacities) to transmit records from the past without altering them, except when the scribe felt sure that he recognized an earlier corruption and attempted—with what he was bound to think was the guidance of Divine inspiration—to emend the text to its correct original state.

Newly written texts, such as those of the religious controversies of the Middle Ages and during the Reformation, often took the form of commentaries on earlier authorities, such as those written by John Duns Scotus and William of Ockham on the *Sententiae* of Peter Lombard, the commentaries on Aristotle and Plato by Christian, Jewish, and Islamic philosophers, and the biblical commentaries of Calvin and Luther.[5] Originality was not prized, and writers would go to great lengths to demonstrate that their ideas came directly out of the authoritative religious, philosophical, or scientific texts of the past. In such an atmosphere, not only was there no motivation for an author to preserve early false starts and rejected byways but there were incentives to hide any biographical evidence that such individual groping toward truth had ever taken place.[6] During the Renaissance, another reason why secular writers discarded drafts and early versions of their poems was the courtier's ideal of *sprezzatura,* an air of pretended scorn for the labor leading to accomplishments, so that courtly poets pretended that they could spin a rhyme or throw off a song with little or no effort. In this atmosphere, it was natural that not only were there few attempts to preserve a record of the ephemeral thoughts writers had rejected in order to move toward their final ideas but such byways of reasoning were often suppressed.

Students of medieval and Renaissance intellectual history will add that the compositions of these eras involved an oral and mnemonic tradition, in which thoughts were first sorted out in the mind before they were committed to quill and ink. Materialistic determinists may observe that we seldom find the notes and preliminary drafts of major works because of the high cost of paper and the value that it undoubtedly had for starting fires on cold mornings. But in the reminiscent fiction of Elizabeth Gaskell's *Cranford* we find recorded the rationale for this destruction, and in the practice of William Godwin, a man of traditional mind who tried to emulate the great thinkers of earlier ages, we find, I believe, the analogue of the Renaissance philosopher. The fifth chapter of Gaskell's *Cranford,* entitled "Old Letters," recounts elderly Miss Matty Jenkyns's performance of what she deems to be her duty of "looking over all the old family letters, and destroying such as ought not to be allowed to fall into the hands of strangers," which include the courtship letters between her parents, letters exchanged by her maternal grandmother and her mother after the birth of Mrs. Jenkyns's children, and those by Matty's deceased older sister. She does so not because of any quality of the letters themselves and certainly not because they contain any scandals or private vices; the letters—which Miss Matty lets her friend read at will—contain nothing of which she or her family need be ashamed. But following age-old tradition, Miss Matty believes simply that people of good taste do not open their hearts or minds to strangers and that since she is the last of her line, no one will survive her who has a right to peruse the intimate correspondence of her family.[7]

William Godwin, in composing both his novels and such works of scholarship and controversy as his *Of Population* (popularly known as his "Answer to Malthus"), would think through each sentence, writing his manuscript in a hand as clear as print, and would compose a three-volume work of fiction at a steady pace, with a regular schedule of writing each day, before sending the manuscript to press with relatively minor corrections and a handful of one- or two-page inserts, along with smaller additions written on the facing blank verso leaves. We know the progress of Godwin's writing from the detailed daily record in his journal, kept from 1788 until just before his death in 1836. (This journal, the property of Lord Abinger, is now on deposit at the Bodleian Library.) There we find a record of how on Sunday, 26 May 1799, Godwin re-sumed his work on *St. Leon* (a philosophical romance published in four volumes in 1800) with page 101. At the beginning of each daily journal entry, Godwin noted the furthest point of his writing, recording his work for this typical week as follows: Monday, 27 May, "St. Leon, p[age] 102"; 28 May, page 104; 29 May, page 106; 30 May, "1 page" (presumably put in those terms because Godwin had scheduled himself for two pages each day); 31 May, "St. Leon, p. 109"; and on Saturday, 1 June, "St. Leon, p. 112/2" (Godwin's indication that he had reached the middle, not the end of page 112). All Godwin's work—on plays, novels, philosophical treatises— was equally systematic. Though he did revise,[8] correcting earlier sections of each work as later parts developed, there was a relatively ordered step-by-step progression to his work, verifiable from his neat manuscripts that clearly served as both rough draft and press copy, which does not correspond to the way Wordsworth, Coleridge, Byron, Shelley, or Keats wrote either poetry or prose.

I envision Godwin's procedure as being close to that of the typical Renaissance writer, moving ahead step by step in the composition of a treatise or tract. Doubtless some did not, but crumpled up page after spoiled page for the tinder box. In Peter Croft's invaluable two-volume compilation *Autograph Poetry in the English Language* (1973), nearly every poetic facsimile he presents in the first volume, devoted to the English poets from the medieval period through the eighteenth century, shows evidence of authorial corrections; a few display extensive revisions. Yet Croft's text makes clear that these surviving holographs themselves are the exception rather than the rule. For several well-known sixteenth- and seventeenth-century poets, including Spenser, Drayton, Marvell, and Vaughan, there are no known surviving autograph manuscripts of their verse. The only poem by Sir Philip Sidney to survive in his autograph did so because it was written in the margin of a book of some value,[9] while poetic holographs of Donne and Ben Jonson survived primarily because they were written as verse letters and thus were filed with the accumulated correspondence of a family occupying "the same spacious house . . . for generations," where, as Peter Croft notes, "it is frequently easier to let papers accumulate than to destroy them."[10]

William Shakespeare was an author of dramas for a repertory theatrical company that must more than once have rehearsed from his original script and from scribal acting copies of his plays to which he added bits of dialogue or even entire scenes during rehearsals or between performances. Yet for Shakespeare, there is—if all the experts agree to accept it—just one autograph scene of three pages in the additions to *Sir Thomas More*, a manuscript that is mainly in the hand of Anthony Munday. For Molière, an equally famous public man of the theater, there is no known holograph. And though at Trinity College, Cambridge, there survive drafts of Milton's *Lycidas* and *Comus*, for a poet as late as Dryden no working drafts survive, and the sole autograph manuscript of one of his poems—his "Heroique Stanzas" on the death of Oliver Cromwell—survived so obscurely that it was first identified in 1966 among the Lansdowne manuscripts in the British Library by a scholar from the University of Padua.

When we turn to prose—excluding letters, which tended to be bundled and stored, if the family had room—we find that examples of autographs and especially of preliminary drafts are especially rare. One prime example of a press-copy manuscript of the sixteenth century is Bodleian MS. adds. c. 165, comprising book 5 of Richard Hooker's *Of the Laws of Ecclesiastical Polity,* transcribed for the press by Benjamin Pullen, Hooker's amanuensis, with added notes, corrections, and revisions in the author's hand—or more correctly *hands,* both his secretary hand and his italic hand. W. Speed Hill, in the second volume of the Folger Library Edition of *The Works of Richard Hooker,* says of this manuscript: "it is one of a handful of Elizabethan manuscripts to have gone through the printing house and survived, and it is certainly the most extensive."[11] As Hill points out, there is a mystery about how this particular part of the press-copy manuscript came to survive, its provenance putatively deriving from either the publisher Edwin Sandys (as Hill suggests, p. xxiv) or the printer John Windet rather than through Hooker's heirs. But in any case, the survival of such press-copy manuscripts is so demonstrably rare that they must usually have been discarded almost as soon as the printing and proofreading had been completed.[12]

Another reason why so few holographs survive from the Renaissance may be that while professional scribes mastered the standard hands of the age that were universally legible to their peers, some of the authors themselves did not. Hill writes: "Pullen's hand is eminently legible, both in italic and secretary, whereas Hooker's displays a characteristic slope and compression that makes his interlinear additions often a puzzle. Indeed, by 1660, if one is to believe Charles Hoole, the art of reading Hooker's script was lost altogether; he comments in *A New Discovery of the Old Art of Teaching Schoole:* 'I, with some others, have bin sorry to see some of that reverend and learned *Mr. Hooker's Sermons* come *in manuscript* to the presse, and not to have been possible to be printed, because they were so scriblingly written, that no body could read three words together in them'" (Hooker, *Works,* 5:xxi–xxii). In an age that prized conformity rather than individuality, the personal hands of authors would give way to the conventionalized handwriting of the professional scrivener. This in itself helps explain the dearth of holographs; then, when the secretary hand went out of use and became difficult to read, those inheriting such scribal manuscripts who had difficulty deciphering the copyists' secretary hands would have valued those manuscripts less because they were *not* in the writing of the famous authors themselves and therefore would have been more likely to discard them.

One of the earliest holograph manuscripts in Oxford, that of William of Malmesbury's *Gesta pontificum,* dating from the decade of 1120 (Magdalen College MS. Lat. 172, on deposit in the Bodleian), provides (as B. C. Barker-Benfield pointed out to me) another interesting example of why occasional earlier holographs survived. According to R. M. Thomson's analysis of this unusually small (pocket-sized) holograph of 106 leaves, which is filled with corrections and revisions later than surviving scribal copies of the first version of this work (1125), this informally written document was clearly the author's personal text, used for the preparation of the revised version of the *Gesta pontificum* (ca. 1135). Moreover, as Thomson indicates in "The 'scriptorium' of William of Malmesbury," William and a few assistants operated an informal scriptorium at their abbey in which William of Malmesbury was himself the most careful and artistic among a group of amateur scribes.[13] His personal copy may, therefore, have been retained for the abbey's collection after scribal copies by his assistants had been sent elsewhere.

Thus, although—as the few surviving autographs suggest—many authors must have revised their work, few of them, their friends, or their heirs felt that the blotted sheets provided anything of interest or value to make them worthy of preservation.[14] Significantly, two of the authors for whom some drafts do survive are Sir Francis Bacon and John Milton, each of whom had a highly developed interest in the New Science and the intellectual developments of his age, leading him to develop attitudes that we now recognize as looking forward toward the following Age of Enlightenment. Most manuscripts that survive from the Renaissance possess the same characteristics as those dating from the late medieval period. After we subtract scribal copies of works from earlier periods that were made for public circulation (and were thus really medieval *books* rather than modern manuscripts), the survivals include many fair copies prepared by the author or an amanuensis for public reproduction; some unpublished plays that may have had a private performance or two and some verses sent as or within letters to particular individuals; many commonplace books; numerous letters on public or state business; a few private diaries, records of travels, and memoirs; and a handful of autobiographies, most by self-made men of bourgeois origins.[15]

The Italians of commercial Lombardy and Tuscany, the leading citizens of which were merchant princes in every sense of that phrase, wrote and collected personalia relating to commoners earlier than people elsewhere in Europe, hoping to create dynasties of the imagination. Dante's compact portraits of his contemporaries in the *Commedia* set the pattern. The personal interests of the Humanists, led by Petrarch, reinforced the attention to individuals and their artifacts. The great manuscript survivals of this age include the holograph of Boccaccio's *Teseida,* a poem of fifteen thousand lines in twelve books of ottava rima, with the author's notes written as holograph glosses. And the Cinquecento saw such great biographical works as Giorgio Vasari's *Lives of the Most Eminent Italian Architects, Painters and Sculptors* . . . (1550) and *The Life of Benvenuto Cellini, written by himself* (1558–62).

Even earlier, dating all the way back to the latter half of the Trecento, were the manuscript collections of Francesco di Marco Datini (1335–1410), the orphaned son of a tavern-keeper in Prato who acquired great wealth by trading in a series of interlocking partnerships in Avignon, Prato, Florence, Pisa, Genoa, Barcelona, and Majorca. Datini hoarded both his commercial and personal manuscripts through the latter half of his life, and at his death in 1410 he left in his home at Prato "not only his 575 voluminous account-books and ledgers (bound in white parchment and headed 'In the name of God and profit') but . . . nearly 126,000 business and private letters" and documents that provide "a glimpse of the daily life of a household of the fourteenth century, the relationship of its members to each other, and especially, of Francesco's own dealings with his active, intelligent, argumentative wife."[16] But the degree to which these Tuscan writers and collectors were ahead of their time in relation to the rest of Europe can be seen from the facts that Cellini's autobiography, though completed in 1562, was not published until 1728 and that in spite of Francesco di Marco Datini's almost preternatural foresight in ordering all his partners and subordinates to keep every document from all branches of his business and ship them to him at Prato, where he bequeathed his house and all the records of his life and business to the commune, this treasure trove remained untouched (except by nibbling rodents) from his death in 1410 until 1870.

English society at this period was little influenced by those who might wish to record their personal achievements instead of relying for terrestrial glory on their dynastic and official positions within the durable feudal, national, and religious institutions. Aside from the stylized personal remarks in such literary genres as the sonnet sequence, writing that was primarily personal—and holograph manuscripts—survived from the Renaissance period more often by accident than by design. The common practice in all writing was to destroy the drafts from which a fair copy had been transcribed, just as a common practice in publishing was to throw away the press-copy manuscript once the printed text was safely proofread.

When the texts of personal letters survive, they are likely to do so in such letterbooks as Folger MS. V.a.321 (into which two scribes copied 140 public and personal documents dating from about the year 1600 into the early seventeenth century). These documents include both public letters on national events and personal letters by Ben Jonson, George Chapman, and the family of Thomas Burgh of Gainsborough.[17] But whether the original occasions that elicited these letters were public or private, most of them had clearly been copied into the letterbook because they provided good models of "how to" petition for redress of a grievance or "how to" court a lady.[18] In the limited world of the English gentry and aristocracy, such letters by known correspondents must have retained some personal interest, but in these scribal copies they had also become published epistolary guides by the same kind of functional shift that in the mid-eighteenth century caused the printer Samuel Richardson to begin a series of "familiar letters" as models to improve the morals and letter-writing skills of servant girls but then turn it into the novel *Pamela*. During the Renaissance, the personal developed into the corporate and the functional; during the Enlightenment, after functionalism had fully developed, it was transformed into imaginative art.

III.

Following the lead of such late sixteenth-century precursors as Montaigne and Bacon, Enlightenment authors came to see greater value in the process of thinking through a problem

and making public the growth and changes in their understanding. For if scientific evidence, reason, and logical persuasion were considered values in themselves, then to show
oneself able to grow and change in the light of extended study
and greater reflection was a sign of an intellect in proper
working order. From the latter half of the seventeenth century
there survive more records of scientific experiments, more
unpolished notes on natural phenomena, more personal
records of every kind of thought and speculation, with the
array of such personal documents in Britain buttressed at one
end by Samuel Pepys's shorthand diary and at the other by
the journals of James Boswell. Between these rise the arches
of familiar letters of such notable epistolarians as Horace
Walpole and William Cowper.

Among these writings some — such as Richard Steele's letters
to his second wife Mary ("Prue"), née Scurlock, and, in America, the remarkable correspondence between John and Abigail
Adams — really do penetrate the barrier between the formal
and the personal and contain genuine revelations of familial
interactions and character unlike those represented in the pol-
ished-for-publication letters of some authors.[19] The manuscripts of the Adams clan also provide a gauge of the geometric
increase in the volume of modern manuscripts in America
when one compares the introduction to L. H. Butterfield's
edition of *Diary and Autobiography of John Adams* with
accounts of two biographical projects involving more recent
figures. Butterfield's first volume of the Adams Papers begins
by noting that

> for more than a century after 1639 [the date of the first
> document in Massachusetts involving one of Abigail
> Adams's ancestors] there remain only a few wills, deeds,
> receipts, printed fast-day proclamations, and scraps of
> correspondence to document the history of a family of
> farmers, maltsters, and holders of town offices who lived
> their lives below the level of historical scrutiny.
>
> Then, in 1775, John Adams (1735–1826) . . . was jolted
> by an earthquake into starting a diary. With this record

of a young schoolmaster's daily thoughts and experiences, the family records may be said truly to begin. Once begun, they were continued with a diligence that is almost staggering to contemplate, and preserved with exemplary care by one generation after another, each of which in turn added to the bulk.[20]

John Quincy Adams (1767–1848), eldest son of John and Abigail and himself sixth president of the United States, added to his father's habit of keeping a diary the additional one of maintaining a letterbook, in which he kept a copy of every letter he sent, as well as those he received. By the death of *his* son Charles Francis Adams (1807–86), the "combined product of [the family's] labors" with the pen was described by Edward Everett Hale as occupying a room lined with bookcases that could be circled in a walk of "a hundred paces more or less." Butterfield continues: "The microfilm edition of the Adams Papers, 1639–1889, runs to 27,464 feet of 35-mm. film. No one has attempted to count the pages or is likely to. If to the records created and accumulated by the three generations of statesmen were added those of Charles Francis Adams' sons, three of whom were extremely articulate and lived well into the present century [one of them was Henry Adams], the total would certainly run to 400,000 pages and perhaps substantially more."[21]

By contrast with this estimate of the size of the archives, dating from 1639 to the early twentieth century and including the papers of several individuals in each of eight generations of one of the most prominent and most literate families in America, we turn to a recent paper by James Thorpe about his research for a biography of Henry E. Huntington (1850–1927), businessman, philanthropist, and collector of fine books and paintings. In "Historical Research: Standards for a Biography of Henry E. Huntington,"[22] Thorpe estimates that the materials for his projected biography of Huntington include some three million documents, ranging from Huntington's own complete business records and correspondence and the diaries and letters of his mother, sister, and one daughter to numerous clippings about him from the public press. Thus, by the estimates of those who knew these archives best, the materials for one prominent businessman with literary interests whose life spanned the second half of the nineteenth century and the first quarter of the twentieth probably outbulk the archives of five or six generations of the Adams family by a proportion of ten or twenty to one. And then, turning to a recent account of a biography of pioneer Hollywood movie producer Samuel Goldwyn (born Schmuel Gelbfisz), we learn that the papers and memorabilia of Goldwyn and his wife Frances fill "two huge vaults at Lion Moving and Storage in Hollywood," though they cover only the later and more successful years of this very *in*articulate man. They contain such ephemeral items as "gin rummy I.O.U.'s from Irving Thalberg and Harpo Marx" and menus of each dinner party the Goldwyns gave and the names of those who attended.[23]

As Thorpe makes clear in his paper, the primary task for a biographer of Huntington—and obviously also for A. Scott Berg's biography of Goldwyn—is to select, first, a perspective from which to view the man and, second, the relevant materials to be examined. This contrasts with the dearth of personal materials for biographies of figures of the English Renaissance, to say nothing of the figures from the medieval and classical periods. Biographers of Shakespeare might well be willing to exchange all the legal and official documents in which he is mentioned for ten long letters from the dramatist to his wife or to an intimate friend dating from the 1590s. The case is almost equally daunting for biographers of figures who lived in the sixteenth century as for those of figures living in the twentieth century: the one has to invent large parts of a life for which no solid evidence exists; the other cannot say a word that may not be contradicted by some extant document that he or she has not had time to examine or has forgotten by the time the research is completed. The editors of the letters of authors of the two periods face similar dilemmas. An edition of T. S. Eliot and his circle could never approximate the scope and depth of *Shelley and his Circle,* for the materials that could be included in such a publication and those necessary to annotate them would be virtually limitless. This is not to say that modern manuscripts of the middle years have been more vigorously studied than those earlier or later, but the chances of success appear best for the period from the 1640s to the 1880s, after the dearth of evidence gave way to more plentiful supplies and before the glut of the later post-Romantic period and the invention of such electronic media as the telephone injected certain distortions in the documentary record that make analysis more difficult.[24]

In the five chapters that follow (corresponding to the second half of the first Lyell lecture and the four subsequent ones I delivered at Oxford) I discuss the principles of manuscript study for that middle period, from the beginning of the Enlightenment to the later phases of the Romantic era. For some ideas and facts, I am indebted to the people whom I credit, but a central concern of the lectures — distinctions in the nature and function of *private, confidential,* and *public* manuscripts and the implications of these differences for the editor, biographer, historian, and literary critic — emerged as I reflected on my years of working with a variety of literary manuscripts, letters and journals, and documents. I believe that if the utility of the distinctions between these three classes of manuscripts becomes more widely understood and accepted, both the study of modern manuscripts themselves and bibliographical and editorial work based on them may become better focused.

INTEREST IN THE PERSONAL

AND THE COLLECTING OF

MANUSCRIPTS

❖

I.
The Growth of Interest in the Personal

Even before the eighteenth century a large proportion of the personal revelations that posterity has thought worthy of publishing and studying came from the bourgeoisie rather than from the gentry and the aristocracy. In northern Europe, many of these introspective writings involve middle-class puritan, evangelical, Quaker—ultimately Augustinian—traditions of spiritual accounting. But the much broader sweep of the increase in the survival of a variety of manuscript records—early drafts of poems, or holograph press-copy manuscripts—reflects the new sense that life and truth reside in *process* rather than simply in its static, completed *product*. The less authority society granted to an immutable Divine order or to an unchanging Reason, the more likely were people to take an interest in tracing the personal growth of remarkable individuals and in the development of their own ideas and those of others under the guidance of their private experience.

Both the accumulation of personal manuscripts and the growing importance of such literary genres as biography, autobiography, memoirs, journals, and letters mark the transformation of society from a cohesive entity, from which the individuals derived their identity and meaning, to the pluralistic yet stereotyped modern commercial society, in which the individual must strive to attain not only a meaningful place but a personal identity as well. In the medieval social order that (owing to cultural lag) persisted virtually intact through the early Renaissance, before the new ideology of the advanced Renaissance thinkers had created imbalances and pressures that led to dramatic social change, individuals had submerged their identity in that of their families, villages, trades, or professions. They did not need to achieve a status in the community; whether peasant or prince, they were born with one and had only to accommodate themselves to its ideals. Social mobility for the bright scions of the lower classes was facilitated by the church, through which talented peasants' sons could receive an education to become priests, and ambitious sons of merchants or landowners might rise to become bishops or cardinals.[1]

So strong was the identification of the individual with family, locale, and profession that a great majority of the surnames that still adorn modern families of European ancestry derive from patronymics (Anderson, ap-Roberts, Fitzmorris, Marovic, Whiting), from professions (Baker, Fletcher, Marchand, Schneider), from place names (Genovese, Hollander, Pforzheimer, York), or from topographical features that identified the family's locale (Bridges, Field, Rougemont, Rivers). Only a minority relate to the characteristics, habits, or achievements of individuals (Long, Strong, Schwarzkopf, Romeo). One of the most common tropes in comic and satirical literature from the medieval to the Romantic period was the naming of fictive comic characters or veiled representations of living people according to their personal characteristics (Volpone, Sir Fopling Flutter, Mrs. Malaprop), both because this mode of naming was a rarity in real life and in order to highlight the egregious aspects of such characters.

The sense of individuality that began to grow in the Renaissance finally became socially dominant in Europe and America during the Romantic period, as "creative imagination" and "self-reliance" replaced "social usefulness" and "good of whole" (often given the shorthand designation "the will of God") as the watchwords of approval and value within the social order. This change approximated that of an earlier era when the values of the old tribes and city-states of the Mediterranean world had given way to individuality in Athens and some other Greek states in the fifth century B.C.E. and in Rome after the fall of the Republic.[2]

When we examine the writings of the English Romantics themselves, we find that growth and development had become watchwords of their art. "The child is the father of the man," wrote Wordsworth, and in his poetry the artist is usually seen looking back over his shoulder or, in one of his most memorable spots of time in the first book of *The Prelude*, facing backwards in a boat as he rows away from his developmental past, only to see it rise up from behind the screen of quotidian concerns and tower over him in an image of luminous but chastening Power (1.357–400; 1850 text). This period gives us the speculative marginalia and the introspective notebooks of Coleridge, as well as the revealing letters of Lamb, Byron, Keats, and Mary Shelley.

In the first edition of *Enquiry concerning Political Justice* William Godwin advocated an ideal of candor that he later practiced in his audacious attempt to tell the whole truth in his *Memoir* of Mary Wollstonecraft's life, but facing a hostile audience, he succeeded only in blackening her reputation.[3] This experience so chastened Godwin (a naturally cautious man) that when he and young Percy Bysshe Shelley began to correspond (in the winter of 1811–12, before they had met), they debated the question of which was best—the Romantic attention to the writer's development, or the older, Renaissance ideal (espoused by Godwin) of suppressing the record of one's early mistakes. On 26 January 1812 Shelley wrote to Godwin:

> You regard early authorship detrimental to the cause of general happiness. I confess that this has not been my opinion even when I have bestowed deep, and I hope

disinterested thought upon the subject: If any man would determine sincerely and cautiously at *every* period of his life to publish books which should contain the real state of his feelings and opinions, I am willing to suppose that this portraiture of his mind would be worth many metaphysical disquisitions.[4]

On 24 February, having proceeded to Dublin to liberate the Irish from their ignorance and subservience by means of his speeches and two pamphlets, Shelley again wrote to Godwin, defending the efficacy of his plan to publish as he thought:

I find that whilst my mind is actively engaged in writing or discussion that it gains strength at the same time that the results of its present power are incorporated; I find that subjects grow out of conversation, and that tho' I begin a subject in writing with no definite view, it presently assumes a definite form in consequence of the method that grows out of the induced train of thought. I therefore write, and I publish because I will publish nothing that shall not conduce to virtue, and therefore my publications so far as they do influence shall influence to good.— (Shelley, *Letters*, 1:259)

On 4 March, Godwin, exasperated by his disciple's naiveté, wrote:

I see no necessary connection between writing and publishing; and, least of all, with one's name. The life of a thinking man, who does this, will be made up of a series of retractions. It is beautiful to correct our errors, to make each day a comment on the last, and to grow perpetually wiser; but all this need not be done before the public. It is commendable to wash one's face, but I will not wash mine in the saloon of the opera-house. A man may resolve, as you say, to present to the moralist and metaphysician a picture of all the successive turns and revolutions of his mind, and it is fit there should be some men that should do this. But such a man must be contented to sacrifice general usefulness, and confine himself to this. Such a

man was Rousseau; but not such a man was Bacon, or
Milton. (Ibid., 1:261)

Godwin's invocation of the names of Bacon and Milton was
not arbitrary, for they were two authors of the English Renaissance who most valued the study of growth and development in their own ideas. They were both highly valued by the
English Romantics partly because their self-consciousness had
helped form the aura of the later ages, Bacon especially through
his influence on the scientific developments of the later seventeenth and the eighteenth centuries and Milton because his
monitoring of his own moral growth and his service in the
larger political world set a standard for poets who would also
be legislators. Godwin was self-conscious enough to keep in
his daily journal a record of his own activities, including even
(if the analysis in an appendix to St. Clair's *The Godwins and
the Shelleys* is correct) his experiences of coition with Mary
Wollstonecraft, as well as a record of his encounters with
significant people, places, books, and public events. Shelley
attempted, as long as he could find compliant publishers, to
make the world the witness to his intellectual and moral
growth. It is not surprising, therefore, that Mary Wollstonecraft Godwin Shelley so applied this dedication to the study
of her father's and husband's careers that she saved almost
every scrap of writing by, to, or about each man and edited
painfully recovered versions of most of Shelley's mature literary efforts, fragments as well as finished works. Without
probing too deeply here into her personal motives, we can see
that she felt that she was performing a service both to the
reading public and to the memory of Shelley by transcribing
all the bits and pieces that she could glean from his chaotic
draft notebooks, and she eventually published most of these
fragments. At the end of the preface to her edition of Shelley's
Posthumous Poems Mary Shelley first names those works that
had "received the author's ultimate corrections" and then
those like "The Triumph of Life," which was "left in so unfinished a state, that I arranged it in its present form with
great difficulty." She then adds:

I do not know whether the critics will reprehend the insertion of some of the most imperfect among these; but I frankly own, that I have been more actuated by the fear lest any monument of his genius should escape me, than the wish of presenting nothing but what was complete to the fastidious reader. I feel that the Lovers of SHELLEY'S Poetry (who know how more than any other poet of the present day every line and word he wrote is instinct with peculiar beauty) will pardon and thank me: I consecrate this volume to them.[5]

In 1839, Mary W. Shelley edited and Edward Moxon published four volumes of Shelley's *Poetical Works;* she revised and expanded the text in a one-volume second edition before the year was out, rather reluctantly including *Queen Mab* complete and adding *Swellfoot the Tyrant* and *Peter Bell the Third* (which she feared might not enhance his reputation). But she took apparent pride in the fact that "in . . . carefully consulting Shelley's scattered and confused papers, I found a few fragments which had hitherto escaped me, and was enabled to complete a few poems hitherto left unfinished. What at one time escapes the searching eye, dimmed by its own earnestness, becomes clear at a future period." Then, alluding to Shelley's very personal late lyrics to Jane Williams, she continues: "By the aid of a friend I also present some poems complete and correct, which hitherto have been defaced by various mistakes and omissions."[6] In 1840 Mary Shelley went on to edit two volumes of Shelley's *Essays, Letters from Abroad, Translations and Fragments,* though in the preface to the latter she admitted: "The first piece in these volumes, 'A Defence of Poetry,' is the only entirely finished prose work Shelley left."[7] The attitude of writers as well as readers toward making public the personal, the fragmentary, and the rejected orts (the very coffee grounds, egg shells, and orange peels) of literature had turned 180 degrees since the early Renaissance, when the polished manuscript of the author himself was often discarded as soon as a work had been properly copied by a professional scribe.

II.
Collections of Personal Manuscripts

Besides the growing cult of the personal, one practical reason why the saving and collecting of manuscripts, especially personal ones, began to flourish was that technological changes in the late eighteenth and early nineteenth centuries increased the number of autograph manuscripts available to collectors. With the spread of literacy and the increased production and decreasing cost of writing paper, more people kept diaries and commonplace books. Improved postal systems enabled even British colonials in India or Australia (or expatriates in Italy) and American travelers in Europe to maintain regular correspondence with their friends and families at home. Whereas Scott opens *The Heart of Midlothian* by recalling the situation of "twenty or thirty years" earlier (i.e., the 1780s), when the Scottish mails had been carried by a horse cart that could travel "with difficulty a journey of thirty miles *per diem*," by 1785 in England (as De Quincey notes in "The English Mail Coach") John Palmer had established the system of stage coaches to carry the mail speedily, in the first three years increasing the postal revenues by almost 50 percent.[8]

But a concurrent series of social and ideological changes also contributed to the growing interest in the personal during the eighteenth and nineteenth centuries. While daily life became more impersonal, and men and women (as Wordsworth lamented) crowded into cities until they lost all personal knowledge of their neighbors, they began to feel a pseudo-personal interest in celebrities—dukes, generals, philosophers, poets, as well as actors, great beauties, notorious criminals, and others who (as Andy Warhol described this phenomenon in our time) became famous for fifteen minutes. The widespread growth of interest in personalia of and about strangers was thus an attempt to hold onto personal relationships that social changes were rendering increasingly tenuous.

The expanding interest in producing and reading biographies and autobiographies occurred as the Industrial Revolution reached its full momentum during the period between

1789 and 1832, the traditional boundaries of the English Romantic period. Ironically, at the same time, the growth of the reading public and the profits that could be realized by publishers who took advantage of this interest in the personal began to transform printing, publishing, and authorship themselves into more standardized and less individual endeavors. During the early nineteenth century, even the writing of biographies and autobiographies was transformed from a labor of love into a business. Boswell's *Life of Samuel Johnson* (1791) and Godwin's *Memoirs of the Author of the Vindication of the Rights of Woman* (1798) were followed by a rash of routine, commercial biographies and life-and-letters projects, such as Southey's major lives of Nelson and John Wesley, his shorter accounts of Marlborough, Wellington, the British admirals, Cromwell, and Bunyan, and his fifteen-volume life and works of William Cowper. In the same way, the confessional or self-justifying autobiography, whether in the vein of Hume's laconic account of his intellectual development or that of Alfieri's Rousseauistic *La vita . . . da suo stesso* (1804), was succeeded by that of William Hayley, who—esteemed by many as a major English poet during the 1780s and 1790s—received an annuity from Henry Colburn for the last twelve years before his death in 1820 on the condition that he leave the bookseller a publishable autobiography.[9] Quasi-personal travel diaries and travel letters became at once popular and commercially successful forms. In this atmosphere, a substantial share of philosophical, political, and literary writing was also shaped to take advantage of the interest in the personal.[10]

Newspapers and magazines also both whetted and profited from the interest in personalia about famous people by articles that gave readers tantalizing glimpses into the daily lives and personal traits of several hundred British celebrities, often publishing engraved portraits, phrenological reports, and eventually lithographed specimens of their handwriting.[11] Graphology and phrenology became popular pseudosciences, and readers sought insight into the minds of their favorite authors not only by reading gossip about their daily lives in the increasingly personal newspapers and magazines but also by viewing their painted portraits in galleries or engraved or lithographed representations of their physiognomies and handwriting in periodicals and in books that gathered such material, as in Finden's famous *Illustrations* to Byron's *Works.*[12]

The public soon began to cherish samples of the authors' own autographs — first in albums, often kept by children whose families were acquainted in literary circles, but eventually through the exchange and purchase of literary and historical autographs. Anonymous readers or "fans" began to covet something personal from their idols — a lock of hair, if possible, or at least a scrap of their handwriting. Few in that period were immune to the emotions associated with such collecting. In 1824, when Thomas Carlyle received a letter from Goethe and obtained a fragment of a letter from Byron, he expressed his enthusiasm to Jane Welsh, then in Scotland, and sent the autographs on for her to see. She responded: "The Autographs you have sent me, have all of them a value . . . but Byron's handwriting — my own Byron's — I esteem, not as a *curiosity* merely, but rather as a relic of an honoured and beloved Friend."[13]

In the mid-nineteenth century, when the fad of autograph collecting degenerated to the clipping of signatures or led to cutting up such literary holographs as Byron's "Oscar of Alva," Shelley's *Laon and Cythna,* and Keats's *Isabella* into small pieces to feed the appetite for examples of the poets' handwriting, it was destructive of manuscript evidence. But the increased monetary value of the handwriting of major writers also helped to preserve early literary drafts and personal letters that might otherwise have been discarded. Yet for every action in human behavior, there tends to be an equal and opposite reaction. Following unpleasant personal revelations about the Romantics, from Coleridge's opium addiction to Keats's "flint-hearted" letters to Fanny Brawne, many Victorian writers grew self-conscious about maintaining their privacy and tried to keep their personal manuscripts from prying eyes. Arnold, Browning, and Tennyson all apparently took steps to destroy parts of the record of their own pasts, and Hardy not only did this but also tried to control the story of his early life by writing his autobiography under his wife's name before destroying much of the evidence about his formative years.[14]

Twentieth-century authors, still surrounded by the enthusiasm for collecting manuscripts, have responded in two opposite directions. Recognizing the interest in their letters and archives, some have tried to preserve them, planning that they be donated or sold to research institutions, while others have tried to prune or destroy the record so that purely personal information, especially information that might prove hurtful to their families or friends, cannot be recovered. Both Somerset Maugham and W. H. Auden, for example, appealed to their correspondents to burn their personal letters. C. S. Lewis, it is reported, was even more hostile to the possibility that the eyes of posterity might intrude on his personal correspondence. Claude Rawson, reviewing three books on Lewis in the *Times Literary Supplement* writes of

> Lewis's custom of burning letters two days after he received them. This was, he explained . . . , not because he didn't value them, but because he didn't wish "things often worthy of sacred silence" to be read by posterity: "For nowadays inquisitive researchers dig out all our affairs and besmirch them with the poison of 'publicity.'" This was not simply a hostility to journalistic investigators. Lewis rarely kept letters . . . from T. S. Eliot and Charles Williams. He also discarded many of his own manuscripts, and for a long time failed even to date his own letters. . . . he disliked . . . the kind of literary criticism which dealt in biographical personality, and was resolutely opposed to "research" and its increasing encroachment on the institutional study of literature.[15]

But the ability of these and other authors to control the fate of their own manuscripts has diminished as the financial rewards to those who preserve and sell such material have risen. At the same time that ordinary people of the early nineteenth century were collecting autographs of the famous living, such

rich, acquisitive manuscript collectors as Frederick North, fifth
earl of Guilford (1766–1827), Dawson Turner (1775–1858),
and Sir Thomas Phillipps (1792–1872) were filling their houses
with other people's manuscripts, in a way that Datini, the
merchant of Prato, had once preserved his own.[16]

III.
Institutional Collecting in America

As large collections of modern as well as classical and medieval
manuscripts began to find their way from private collectors
or their heirs into major research institutions in Britain and
America, they brought fame and gratitude to their donors and
prestige to the accepting institutions. Soon the established
national and older university libraries and museums were em-
ulated by newer or less prestigious institutions, some backed
by public funds, which sought to acquire important archives
and collections. Most research libraries in America owed their
initial excellence to the enthusiasm of private individuals who
collected books and manuscripts in specialized fields and then
sold, donated, or bequeathed their collections to these institutions. Some collectors found ways to build fine collections
out of materials that would now be recognized as part of
Britain's heritage. The libraries of J. Pierpont Morgan, Henry
Folger, and Henry E. Huntington featured the literary manuscripts of British authors. William L. Clements, of Bay City,
Michigan, who was interested in the American War of Independence, bought up the papers of several British generals
who had commands in America during the conflict, making
the Clements Library at the University of Michigan a center
for an interesting passage in British diplomatic and military
history.[17]

Eventually, some of the universities in the United States
realized that they had begun too late to collect literary and
historical archives to compete with the older institutions on
the same terms. Instead of waiting years and courting private
collectors, they began to raise their own money to compete

directly for the custody of the papers of noteworthy individuals and the archives of important historical and cultural institutions when they first went on the market. Sometimes they bought these records from the heirs of noteworthy writers or, in certain cases, from the writers while they were still alive; even more frequently, in the United States, lesser-known writers would receive tax deductions for donating such materials to an institution.

Among other examples, we find that in the 1930s and 1940s, under the prodding of Professors T(homas) W. Baldwin and Harris F. Fletcher of the Department of English, the University of Illinois at Urbana-Champaign became a major collector of books related to Shakespeare and Milton. During the 1950s, the university's activity increased in other areas after Gordon N. Ray, head of the Department of English, suddenly developed an interest in buying primary materials. Collecting for the library at Illinois, inspired and initially guided by Baldwin and rejuvenated by Ray—who were both at the time book buyers of modest means—was at first carried on with as little publicity as possible to avoid raising the market prices. (For years, the Milton Collection at Illinois lacked only the first edition of *Comus* but never told this to outsiders, lest the dealers compete among themselves for a copy to sell to the collection. Baldwin and Fletcher simply waited until one was offered at a reasonable price.) But when Gordon Ray inherited additional money after his father's death in 1956, he himself became a leading collector of literary books and manuscripts and illustrated books that are now part of the Pierpont Morgan Library. Spending his summer holidays on book-buying expeditions, he was efficiently systematic in acquiring books for the university as well: his characteristic mode was to visit the bookshops of Britain with a copy of the *Cambridge Bibliography English Literature* marked with the holdings of the Illinois library and to ask the dealers to quote to the library any books not already marked. He also, however, committed a few acts of real bravura, such as buying for the university an entire roomful of books at a shop in Penzance.[18]

Such buying in bulk could turn up some pleasant surprises.

Jack Stillinger, who arrived at Illinois in the fall of 1958 as a Keats specialist, tells of the discovery of the two missing manuscripts of the *Autobiography* of John Stuart Mill. (In 1958, the only manuscript of the work that was known to exist was at Columbia University.)[19] In that year, the Illinois Library purchased *en bloc* the library of Professor Jacob H. Hollander (1871–1940), who had taught economics at the Johns Hopkins University. The second volume of the checklist of Hollander's collection was devoted entirely to manuscripts, most of them letters listed by author, recipient, and date. After scanning pages of entries beginning "Autograph letter," those purchasing the collection for Illinois failed to notice that the entry for manuscripts under "Mill, John Stuart" began "Autobiography." When the collection arrived at Urbana and the crates were unpacked, the manuscript was discovered. Gordon Ray, then provost of the university, fresh from examining the manuscript, announced the discovery at a meeting of the university senate that afternoon. A professor leaving the senate meeting happened to meet Jack Stillinger and told him of the discovery, and Stillinger, whose special training under Hyder Rollins at Harvard had been in editing nineteenth-century manuscripts, went to Ray that same afternoon and asked for the opportunity to work with the manuscript. Thus did he become a specialist in Mill as well as in Keats. While doing research for his edition of *The Early Draft of John Stuart Mill's Autobiography* (1961), Stillinger located the catalog of Sotheby's sale in which it had first been sold and found there listed not only the Illinois and Columbia manuscripts of the *Autobiography* but also a third, unknown manuscript of it. He wrote a letter of inquiry that was published in the *Times Literary Supplement* asking for news of the whereabouts of this third manuscript, to which Dr. Frank Taylor, of the John Rylands Library, replied that because he had been poking around among manuscripts in Hodgson's salerooms, the Rylands Library had purchased it just eight days before the letter appeared in *TLS*. This proved to be the press copy, transcribed for the press from the Columbia manuscript.[20] This anecdote suggests how rapidly research materials may be put into use after they are acquired by a research institution with a large faculty stimulated by a system that encourages and rewards scholarly publication.

But Illinois, though personally dear to me, obviously did not make the same splash in the market for British books and literary manuscripts that was made by the University of Texas at Austin under the aegis of Harry Ransom. Texas preferred to achieve the maximum publicity by flaunting its wealth in the public auction rooms.[21] Nor was there a dearth of more modestly financed but imaginative efforts to establish major collections of literary manuscripts. Many years ago, Arthur Freeman, now of Bernard Quaritch, told me how soon after he had published his first volume of poems (and while still a student at Harvard), he received an ingratiating letter from a friend at the University of Buffalo (later the State University of New York at Buffalo) persuading him to send him the manuscript of his poetic volume. Flattered, he had done so, and the man at Buffalo had then proceeded to deposit it with the twentieth-century literature collection in the Lockwood Library. By the time he told me the story, Freeman—then in the rare-book trade—realized that the Buffalo library had hit upon a marvelous scheme to end up with the earliest manuscripts of a whole generation of young writers, from which the staff could later sort out the ones who proved to be important. Freeman also relates that Howard Gotlieb, at Boston University (where Freeman taught), used to send out similar letters and netted not only the papers of movies stars such as Bette Davis but also those of Günter Grass shortly before he won the Nobel prize.[22]

The recent competition for unique archival research materials has engaged the attention of more and more university administrators, with the result that the financial rewards to some pack-rat writers have increased substantially. In 1984 the University of Illinois at Urbana purchased the archives of the American poet and translator W. S. Merwin (b. 1927) for $185,000. When the university announced the purchase, the archive was described as including "unpublished works, notes, letters, ideas for poems, personal correspondence and other literary papers." The chancellor of the Urbana campus was quoted as saying that the acquisition "will serve as a unique national resource," and the president of the university noted with pride that the collection "appears to contain virtually every original piece of manuscript that the poet produced in the last 40 years." In this age, so many writers are self-conscious about the potential for fame and fortune in the scraps from their writing tables that they do keep every draft, copy, and proof of each poem or novel during its genesis. A few years ago a friend of mine who had then self-published two slim volumes of verse phoned me to lament having accidentally thrown an intermediate version of a poem into the wastebasket, thus rendering that poet's archives incomplete!

The interest of American research institutions in preserving archives of writers, publishers, politicians, and other public figures, and even of teachers and scholars, has led to the preservation of many important papers. But in a few documentable cases, the distaste of the British for the American collectors has led to the destruction of others. I cite an example that, though published, is perhaps not so well known that it cannot bear repeating. Ian Bruce, in his 1951 book *The Nun of Lebanon: The Love Affair of Lady Hester Stanhope and Michael Bruce,* relates how one group of letters by Lady Hester Stanhope came to the British Museum in the 1930s (before either Illinois or Texas could be blamed).

At a sale of the effects of Stowe House, a Buckingham tradesman bought a number of sacks filled with letters and documents. A lady of the parish, fearing that these papers would fall into the hands of the Americans, bought the lot. She then started to distribute the sacks in the neighbourhood, giving the Rector some for the benefit of the Church finances. The Rector in due course found that his sacks contained the confidential correspondence received by the Duke of Buckingham while he was the Colonial Secretary during 1866–68. [The Rector] describes this correspondence as of some interest, amusing as well as sometimes surprising. The Rector also found the twelve letters written by Hester Stanhope to Sir

Thomas Grenville. In the meantime the Squire had burnt all his sacks and the school-mistress was busy burning hers every time she lit her fire. The Rector rescued what he could and eventually his church funds benefited by fifty pounds and the British Museum bought what was left.[23]

IV.
Self-censorship and Technological Censors

In an atmosphere where all writers and public figures realize that their papers can fall into the hands of collectors and research institutions, rather than ladies of the parish determined to save them from "the Americans," it seems to me unlikely that the materials preserved today will have the same character as those surviving from the eighteenth and early nineteenth centuries, before such self-consciousness set in. The archives of twentieth-century poets and even of presidents and prime ministers—no matter how complete those collections are said to be by those selling them—are apt to lack many of the values that such earlier archives as the Bodleian Shelley manuscripts have. As self-conscious authors become their own archivists and prepare their papers for the day that scholars and critics will go through their drafts and letters, they will be less likely to keep anything that they feel might reflect badly on them. The drafts and correspondence files may yield no surprises for the researcher, or they may even have been seeded with false evidence of interesting roads not taken to intrigue scholars. Though the destruction of documentary evidence viewed by writers or their heirs as potentially embarrassing has always been a possibility and has sometimes occurred, most writers in the early nineteenth century were usually too busy living their own lives and as yet unaware of the consequences of modern literary and biographical research to manufacture false documentary evidence for posterity. Even when they attempted to do so, the small runs of handmade paper with dated watermarks and other evidence that yields to scientific methods of dating often enable us to sort out the truth.

Countess Teresa Guiccioli's collection of her letters to Lord Byron, for example, contains some passages that she later tried to suppress by rewriting key words. Having declared, both for legal reasons and because of attitudes toward sexual freedom changed later in the nineteenth century, that she and Byron had never been lovers, but merely good friends, la Guiccioli tried to disguise the evidence of her sexual relations with Byron and other facts without destroying any of her or Byron's letters. But in most cases, careful analysis of her manuscripts can disentangle fact from fiction, and if we cannot always restore the original words that she changed, we can at least identify the subject matter in the passages she thought necessary to revise. Her alterations, rather than hiding the facts, call attention to the very passages that she found too revealing, and they thus *help* the biographical scholar to assess the significance of some passages that might otherwise seem perfectly innocuous. I give just one example: When discussing the result of a visit to her doctor, Teresa Guiccioli wrote to Byron (as her Italian text has been translated for *Shelley and his Circle*): "I saw Rima—who assured me that my illness is only superficial—it cannot have any consequences and will not be any impediment to my having children.—If you ceased to love me, I would no longer desire any of this, but instead I would consult the Doctors for the speediest and least painful way to die.—" In going over this letter in later years, Teresa Guiccioli altered the phrase "ad avere figli" ("to having children") to "a ben vivere" ("to living well"), thereby removing from the letter the clear evidence of her sexual relationship with Byron.[24] A modern author intent on changing the record in a similar vein might well be able to rewrite the entire letter and destroy the original without giving the scholar any certain clue as to what happened.

Besides the psychological barriers to candor that arise from the awareness by modern writers that their manuscripts have a good chance of being preserved, read, and even published by scholars and journalists, two technological changes may affect the record of manuscript evidence. The papers surviving from the Edwardian period to the present may prove to be less revealing than those of the eighteenth and nineteenth centuries because of the invention of the telephone, for (as an older friend remarked to me in the spring of 1964 when I expressed an undue interest in the nature of personal relations between Shelley and Jane Williams) the use of the telephone will put an end to certain kinds of evidence about the nature of relationships between friends and lovers, since fewer of the communications between them now leave a paper trail.[25]

Another technological advance that may already have affected the level of candor in some kinds of writing is the use of the typewriter. Although there is not room here to explore this question, someone should ponder the effects that the use of the typewriter has had on the nature of writers' initial inscriptions, both public and private, whether or not they composed directly on the machine. What were the effects of Virginia Woolf's use of it in writing some literary works, especially since her drafts show her to be such an indifferent typist? Or what about such authors as Henry James, Thomas Hardy, and James Joyce, who dictated parts of their fiction (and sometimes their correspondence) to be typed by others? Can a writer be personal in a letter dictated to another, typed up, and then corrected by the author? In asking these questions, I am thinking not only about the new potentialities for verbal and other textual errors but of changes in the psychology of composition in the two modes—direct and mechanical—which might be best investigated while there are writers alive who have personally experienced the transition from one to the other. Beyond the chance for a different kind of textual error that can be caused by the juxtaposition of certain letters on the keyboards of various early brands of typewriter, or the potential for a skilled typist to reverse certain letters because the fingers on one hand found their mark sooner than the fingers on the other (technical topics that, like the vagaries of monotype composition, are worth investigation as part of the textual criticism of works in the late nineteenth and the twentieth century), what are the subtle effects of typing personal communications—love letters, for example, or private memoirs? May not the very intervention of a machine and the printlike appearance of the typescript encourage the writer to think in terms of potential readers beyond the addressee and therefore to alter the style to one less intimate and more public?

To summarize: The Romantics valorized growth and experience, an ideal that succeeded the ostensibly scientific and objective values of the Enlightenment. This change in perspective altered the production and uses of manuscripts, which became more important both to readers and to the writers themselves, who used the medium of "paper doomed to perish" to record their inmost thoughts, either for their own later use or for perusal by a few intimates. As the public at large came to be more appreciative of the personal manuscripts of writers and other celebrities, valuing and purchasing them, the survival rate of such artifacts increased greatly. But Victorian and modernist writers, seeing the uses to which such personalia had been put by biographers and editors, became increasingly self-conscious about the reactions of this potential readership, sometimes destroying or pruning their archives to maintain their privacy.

Some attempted to build a manuscript record to vindicate themselves to posterity, leaving purportedly "private" accounts of themselves and their contemporaries that were intended for publication after their enemies were no longer in a position (as reviewers, for example) to answer them. Thus, for some the private letter or diary became an unacknowledged mode of publication, quite unlike that of the public press and equally unlike that of the literary texts circulated in the manuscript anthologies and commonplace books of the Middle Ages and the early Renaissance. The purpose of these modern manuscripts was to seem unpremeditated and candid, while actually constituting a new class of art akin to but ostensibly less artistic than published autobiographies and memoirs, or volumes of correspondence published by the authors during their lifetime, or openly prepared for publication after their death.

In the next three chapters, I shall try to show that however much the attitude toward personal manuscripts has changed between the early nineteenth century and our own time, there remains for both the Romantics and authors today a clearly definable boundary between manuscripts prepared for transmission to the public and those written for the eyes of the writer and, at most, a limited number of friends or acquaintances. Moreover, there is also a clear demarcation between a literary work left in manuscript and the printed version of that same text.

PRIVATE, CONFIDENTIAL, AND

PUBLIC MANUSCRIPTS

❖

I.
Types of Manuscripts Differentiated

All manuscripts, I believe, can be classified as either *public, confidential* (or *corporate*), or *private* (or *personal*). *Public* manuscripts include both formal compositions prepared for publication or other transmission (such as lectures, sermons, treatises, histories, poems, and novels) and compositions fulfilling formal or official functions within a social structure. Public manuscripts record texts that their authors expect or hope will be made accessible to a multiplicity of readers whom the authors do not know and who, at least initially, might have little or no personal interest in the writers themselves; the intended audience is made up of people concerned either with the official or public positions that the writers occupy or with the intellectual, informational, or aesthetic attributes of their writing.

Private, or *personal,* manuscripts, on the other hand, are addressed to specific people, selected in advance, whom the writers know—or hope—will take personal interest in them. Some documents may be intended only for the eyes of the writer (e.g., a private diary or aide-mémoire) or for the eyes of one other person (e.g., a love letter). (That the writer of such a private letter need not be acquainted with the recipient can be seen in the very private letters that Claire Clairmont, among others, wrote to Lord Byron in the hope of meeting him and establishing a personal relationship.)[1] Besides diaries and love letters, other strictly private documents might include marginalia in the writer's own books; or notes written in books owned by friends that are meant to serve as personal communications, such as the love letter Byron wrote to Teresa Guiccioli in her copy of Madame de Staël's *Corinne;*[2] or Coleridge's marginalia calling attention to the beauty and significance of various passages in books belonging to Charles Lamb.[3] *Private* manuscripts might also include some kinds of professional reports, such as a physician's diagnosis, a lawyer's confidential legal opinion, or even perhaps—historians reading this can judge—off-the-record communications between government officials in which the writer (perhaps a trusted friend of the recipient) hopes to correct or supplement official reports on a subject. A category of private manuscripts important to students of literature but also relevant to others fields is the rough drafts and intermediate revises that represent stages in the gestation of a written text between its original inception and its publication or other public presentation.

Of wider circulation than the strictly private document are *confidential,* or *corporate,* manuscripts, not intended for the eyes of a wide and diverse readership, but addressed to a specific group of individuals all of whom either are personally known to the writer or belong to some predefined group that the writer has reason to believe share communal values with him or her: an audience that will receive the communication in the spirit that corresponds to the purpose of its composition. Such confidential communications may be friendly and sympathetic or angry and accusatory. Often the writer of an angry remonstrance intends the recipient, charged with some breach of morals or good manners, perhaps, or a betrayal of friendship, to show or send copies of the letter to mutual friends so that they may judge the merits of the case between writer and addressee. Other confidential documents would include memos to the writer's partners in a law firm or business or to members of a university department or personal staff; they would also include readers' reports to a publishing house. Such documents, since they are not meant for random dissemination, are often written without concern for the laws of libel (for example) or the writer's good name with the public at large or with posterity. This is why many political and business scandals begin when some such confidential or corporate documents are made public.

II.
Categories Determined by Authorial Intentions

The distinctions I have made between private, confidential, and public manuscripts all depend upon the social intentions of the writer. But it is easy to lose sight of these distinctions. Not only are the intentions of the writers themselves often ambiguous or ambivalent but readers often confuse the distinctions between personal and public documents by violating the intentions of the writer. For example, most of the private manuscripts that concern us as students of bibliography, literature, history, or political science have already been made available to a wider public, and where they have not, our work is aimed at making them so available.

In some cases a manuscript that begins as a public or confidential document becomes more personal through the course of its history. The journal kept by Robert Falcon Scott on his ill-fated expedition to the South Pole was an official log of a naval expedition and, as such, a *confidential* document; but like diaries kept by political prisoners or those marooned or cast adrift by shipwrecks or plane crashes, it surely became also a personal account of Scott's efforts and disappointments, as well as a *public* record for posterity of the experience of the writer and his co-sufferers.[4] This document was at once *private* (for Scott's next of kin), *corporate* (for his superior officers), and a *public* apologia for his life. Like letters put into bottles and thrown into the sea, such documents written *in extremis* are often unshaped and ragged when judged by the rules of art, even the art of the published memoir, or

journal. The style of these multipurpose journals also contrasts, moreover, with the unguarded candor or loquacity of
most diaries kept by private individuals for their own personal
consultation—Samuel Pepys's diary in cipher being the epitomizing example—and those that are later prepared for publication, at which time the diarist almost invariably heavily
revises many of the entries.

In most instances, however, the daily routine of keeping a
diary, which usually includes unguarded comments about
those closest to the writer, dictates that it shall be a private
document. If like William Godwin's journal a diary contains
few personal revelations, it may be so laconic as to remain a
puzzle to all but a few persistent scholars.[5] But it may be as
garrulous as Joseph Farington's or as mendacious as I believe
Benjamin Robert Haydon's manuscript diary to be without
destroying the distinction between public and private.[6] So long
as writers do not prepare manuscripts for publication by editing the text and obliterating passages that they feel place
them in a bad light or contradict their later, more considered
opinions, such documents are much more revelatory than any
published diary or one quasi-published by being totally recopied for an imagined posterity. Sometimes, as with the *Diary
of Henry Crabb Robinson,* we are granted an opportunity to
read both what the diarist put down in the first instance and
how he retold the same story in a manuscript memoir based
on a redaction of the diaries.[7]

Anne Frank's *Diary of a Young Girl* might seem to provide
one of the purest examples of a private document made public
by accident. On 12 June 1942, the day Anne Frank received
the diary as a birthday present, she wrote in it: "I hope I shall
be able to confide in you completely, as I have never been able
to do in anyone before, and I hope that you will be a great
support and comfort to me."[8] And in a preface to the French
translation, Daniel-Rops observes that at the age of thirteen
Anne Frank had not yet arrived at a self-consciousness like
that of an adult author, who "poses before the mirror and
thinks of posterity. She didn't give a damn for posterity!"[9]
More recently, however, there have been suggestions that the

text of the original diary was edited and altered before publication by Anne Frank's father, that what millions have read is not the unvarnished truth as young Anne Frank experienced it. Exploring this subject in *The Diary of Anne Frank: The Critical Edition,* the editors and various forensic experts conclude that the story related in the diary is authentic, but they note that changes were made during the diary's transition from a private to a public document.[10] Sometime after 11 May 1944, Anne Frank, who hoped for a career as a journalist after the war, began revising the diary into a fictional account called "The Secret Annexe," changing the names of persons and rearranging the order of events recorded in the original diary itself, parts of which are missing and have been replaced by the revised version, written on loose sheets (pp. 60–62). After the war, Anne's father Otto Frank, partly in deference to the prudishness of his Dutch publisher and to the sensitivity of the publishers of the German translation and partly out of respect for his dead wife, omitted a few passages and phrases that spoke of Anne's menstruation, her fights with her mother, and her hatred of the Germans.

Even had none of these minor changes been made, we would have to concede that the very nature of the diary was changed when the original document (which began as an entirely private record, not intended for the eyes of any other person) *was* mediated to a public of millions through the efforts of Frank's father, her Dutch editors, and translators around the world, who delivered its intimacies in the colloquialisms of many languages. The events relating to the Holocaust, of which Anne Frank was at first a naive witness and at last a victim, were such as to give her record a particularly *public* impact, which in turn made the author a public figure whose childhood letters to an American pen pal before she went into hiding were a much-sought treasure sold at public auction and bid on by collectors and institutions interested in Holocaust memorabilia.[11]

Thus publication and other circumstances can clearly transform a *private* manuscript into a *public* one. Does the very change in status from private to public alter the fundamental character and meaning of a document even if no massive editorial changes or questionable translations accompany the transformation? Private texts are demonstrably treated as if they were public ones whenever the writer, the recipient, or the subject matter gains such fame or notoriety as to arouse the interest of scholars, students, collectors, dealers, curators, or just "fans." But does this apparent change in status alter the basic nature of private texts in such a way that they can be lumped with texts their authors prepared as public documents? Does the mere fact that twenty, or two hundred, or twenty million people are interested in reading the private thoughts of a statesman or poet or martyr change the status of what was conceived as a private communication? There are all kinds of private events of, say, the fourteenth or the nineteenth century that were so common and routine that no reader of that time would have been interested in a diary depicting only the round of contemporary daily life; we, however, may find this routine sufficiently quaint or informative to study and annotate in order to help our contemporaries recover the flavor of a bygone age. In reading and studying these private documents, do we risk committing fundamental scholarly fallacies if we fail to make distinctions between them and public documents with regard to the intentions of the authors and their possible range of effects on readers? Should editors and scholar-critics use different procedures for analyzing and editing private and confidential manuscripts from those they employ in presenting public documents, texts intended by their authors to be read by larger and less clearly defined audiences, including such catchall groups as "the reading public" and "posterity"?

We can imagine—in fact, many of us know—someone who is at this moment quietly writing a novel or long poem that will never be published and will remain a document read only by the author and a few friends. Is such a work to be classified with private letters and journals? I think not, in most cases. Authors who intend that their work be published write with that end in view. By the same logic, when a personal letter is published, it does not thereby become a public document, but simply a published personal text. I have heard of incidents in which a love letter written to an undergraduate and meant sincerely as a private communication was itself so egregious or was sent to such a callous, insensitive person that its contents became public knowledge throughout a dormitory or college, or perhaps the letter was posted on a bulletin board for the amusement of passers-by. The same thing can happen to confidential letters of a corporate nature. Under a former editor of an American scholarly journal, the editor's annual reports formed the staple amusement at the sponsoring association's intimate annual meetings in New York. There the editor quoted, with sarcastic asides, the risible parts of letters of would-be contributors from all over the world. Editors of newspapers may have taught their correspondents to be more circumspect when the papers published whatever they wished from the incoming mail as letters to the editor, but a learned journal with a limited constituency cannot afford to hold up to public ridicule the communications of enthusiastic non-academics from North America and Britain or dedicated teachers from Third World countries who submit papers to the judgment of the academics on a journal's editorial board. Any recording secretary who has tried to revise for publication the language of the documents and comments that constituted the substance of a closed meeting of a committee or board of directors will appreciate the nature of such confidential communications and how they differ from those in the public sphere.

In determining what correspondence is *nonpublic*, that is, either *private* or *confidential*, the degree of friendship or intimacy between the writer and addressee is less important than whether or not a letter is meant primarily for the eyes of one other person or for the eyes of a particular collegial group. When the Shelleys wrote letters to such close personal friends as Leigh and Marianne Hunt, or John and Maria Gisborne, they expected that all the adult members of the family household would read them; but as is obvious from the kinds of complaints and gossip about other mutual friends that these letters contain, they did not expect these letters to be shared beyond that closed circle. When Percy Bysshe Shelley wrote, on the other hand, a series of travel letters to Thomas Love Peacock describing the scenery and art of Italy, he knew and intended that Peacock would share these letters with Thomas Jefferson Hogg and other English friends. It seems clear, moreover, that Shelley and Mary Shelley planned, after excising the small amount of innocent but personal matter from these letters, to publish them in a travel book, as they had revised for publication letters and journal entries about their earlier travels in *History of a Six Weeks' Tour* (1817). While their travel letters to Peacock (and some also to Thomas Jefferson Hogg) are not quite public documents in their manuscript form, they have large sections that can be considered public and not only could be but were published with their approval and without substantive revision.[12]

Byron likewise addressed communications to John Murray that he knew and intended that his publisher would share with the circle of visitors to his upper front room on Albemarle Street. Byron, whose sense of privacy was not as highly developed as Shelley's, shared accounts of his amatory adventures in Venice so intimate as to shock Thomas Moore, not because of the adventures themselves but because Byron had made Murray and his bourgeois circle privy to them. Moore, the son of a Dublin grocer, sounds very snobbish as he disapproves of Byron sending letters about his intrigues "to Murray, the bookseller—a person so out of his caste & to whom he writes formally, beginning 'Dear Sir' "; yet Moore was questioning not Murray's social class but the sheer number and indiscriminate character of the audience invited to read Byron's *confidential* correspondence. Moore himself published only censored versions of Byron's letters to him and then apparently destroyed the manuscripts so that their *private* communications could remain private.[13] Since Byron knew that Murray was not discreet, he certainly wrote to his bookseller with a larger audience in mind than when he wrote to his sister Augusta or to Moore, John Cam Hobhouse, and Douglas Kinnaird, the correspondents to whom he addressed his most purely private letters.

From this point in my discussion, the word *letters* will refer to *personal,* or *private,* communications as I have defined them—meant to be read only by the recipient and perhaps the recipient's household or intimates. I shall employ the term *epistles* to denominate missives that seem to express the writer's personal feelings or beliefs but are directed at a larger audience and intended to be read by or to those who may be interested in learning about the writer's ideas and feelings or of events in his or her life. *Epistles,* or *confidential* or *corporate* communications, would include—besides Byron's gossipy missives to Murray—the New Testament epistles by St. Paul or others to the congregations of various churches, as well as such modern equivalents as the xerographically reproduced annual Christmas letters with which some Americans rehearse for a large and far-flung community of friends and relatives, with their spouses and children, the family's activities during the past year.

III.
Artful and Artless Documents

Epistles that individuals address to select groups or institutions, like all other forms of *confidential* composition, blend expressions of personal feeling with an artistic component that fulfills a need to impress or mollify, to persuade or ingratiate themselves with the chosen corporate audience. For example, the letters pleading for remission of punishment for capital crimes that Natalie Zemon Davis has explored in *Fiction in the Archives: Pardon Tales and Their Tellers in Sixteenth-Century France* reveal various levels of individuality and candor.[14] Clearly, as in letters of complaint that seek the redress of lesser grievances than those subject to a sentence of capital punishment, the art involved is the art of persuasion, which often depends on telling a believable story that puts the writer in a good light. Such letters, as Davis points out, are often cooperative efforts between the ostensible or nominal author and his or her friends, a scribe, and perhaps legal counsel. But they often reveal very personal things as well, especially when they seek to expand upon or broaden the interpretation of laws, rather than merely take advantage of legal precedent.

We are all aware of the artistry and rhetoric that are—or can be—involved in the most personal and most intimate letters, such as those by children at college asking their parents for extra spending money, or by a lover trying to persuade a beloved to keep an indiscreet tryst. Thus, again, the level of self-conscious artistry of a document bears little relationship to the intimacy between writer and recipient, or to the extent of the intended audience. A pair of notes scribbled on a scrap of paper and exchanged in an American courtroom between a defendant and his lawyer—the most private of communications—may be totally artless, while an equally private letter—proposing marriage or declining to accept such a proposal—may be a masterpiece of rhetorical art. A communication that is *confidential,* in that the writer does not expect to find its contents broadcast to others besides the addressee (such as a note to the post office asking that mail be held while the writer is on vacation), may be in a style both completely impersonal and totally without self-conscious art; on the other hand, an author's cover letter for a novel submitted to a publisher may evidence more art than the accompanying fiction.

But lest we suppose that only private or confidential communications can be artless, we must consider for a moment the levels of art in public writings. These can, on occasion, be virtually artless. I am not speaking of government reports, which are (like much academic prose) written in a diction and according to formulas and models approved within the writer's profession or discipline. In his essay "Outside Literature" (1922), Joseph Conrad speaks of the difference between imaginative literature and the "Notices for Mariners," which provide in very literal, "clear and concise" prose "information of an ideal accuracy, such as you do not find in the prose of the works on science, which is mainly imaginative and often solemnly mystifying."[15] The most artless examples of public texts that I can imagine are the original versions of the news reports on daily financial transactions and business statistics that record such things as the rise and fall of prices of currencies and farm commodities. Though we think of these data as coming over a teletype or computer screen or from a radio station, the earlier act of writing or typing these figures onto a form (and correcting them, if the pen miswrote or there was a typing error) created in the first instance the simplest kind of manuscript that is intended for publication.

Such public manuscripts may be laconic and cryptic, as well as artless, in the way that many of the most intimate private manuscripts are. But the distinctions between the levels of audience envisioned by the writers remains crucial, as the Securities and Exchange Commission in the United States recognizes. People who work on Wall Street and other financial markets can go to jail if they do not observe the distinctions between confidential, private, and public communications. Because inside information about the value of stocks traded in the public markets can be worth a good deal to the possessors of it, those privy to confidential information are not allowed to trade, or to advise their friends to trade, in the stocks likely to be affected by that transaction until the news is made public, so that everyone owning or thinking of buying the stock is made aware of its new trading conditions. On a regulated stock market, confidential information must be made public before it may be transmitted privately. Though most such tips are now given by telephone or in face-to-face conversations, rather than in manuscripts, the situation illustrates clearly the distinctions between confidential, private, and public communications.

IV.
Distinguishing Types of Correspondence

Editions of the letters of a literary or political figure usually include within a single chronological sequence two or three different kinds of documents—personal letters, confidential epistles, and public statements in epistolary form. The question arises whether this is always the best method of proceeding. Given the validity of the distinctions in authorial intentions, which are usually clear to the editor who deals with the full range of a writer's correspondence, it should be possible for editors to indicate in their notes the level of intimacy to which each letter seems to belong—whether Byron, for example, meant his sentiments to be held as strictly private, communicated to a limited confidential circle, or made public through a recognized chain of gossip, or even through actual publication, in whole or in part. Such signposts might better enable critics and biographers to probe the differing levels of rhetoric at work in a particular correspondence and to evaluate the candor and the range (and limits) of the relevance of the contents of different letters. Though there are many subjective factors at work, sometimes too many to allow one to arrive at a satisfactory alternative method, some issues ought to be addressed by the editors in their introductions and annotations that would guide readers in evaluating the apparently contradictory evidence that inevitably appears in the letters of any particular writer.

For example, almost every edition of a writer's so-called letters contains a few that were sent, not to individuals, but to the public press—the *Examiner,* the *Morning Chronicle,* the *Times,* the *Athenaeum*—and these differ in kind from both the private letters to friends and the confidential epistles to publishers or business correspondents. I take the following succinct example from Rupert Hart-Davis's edition of *The Letters of Oscar Wilde:*

To the Editor of Truth

[*Early January 1890*]   *16 Tite Street*

Sir, I can hardly imagine that the public are in the very smallest degree interested in the shrill shrieks of "Plagiarism" that proceed from time to time out of the lips of silly vanity or incompetent mediocrity.

However, as Mr James Whistler has had the impudence to attack me with both venom and vulgarity in your columns, I hope you will allow me to state that the assertions contained in his letter are as deliberately untrue as they are deliberately offensive.

The definition of a disciple as one who has the courage of the opinions of his master is really too old even for Mr Whistler to be allowed to claim it, and as for borrowing Mr Whistler's ideas about art, the only thoroughly original ideas I have ever heard him express have had reference to his own superiority over painters greater than himself.

It is a trouble for any gentleman to have to notice the lucubrations of so ill-bred and ignorant a person as Mr Whistler, but your publication of his insolent letter left me no option in the matter.

I remain, sir, faithfully yours

OSCAR WILDE[16]

The texts of communications of this kind must usually be based on printed rather than manuscript sources; if so, the exact date of composition is often unknown, and the public letter must often be dated approximately (as in this case), with the *terminus a quo* being the date of the event or publication that provoked the missive and the date of publication itself providing the *terminus ad quem*. Such statements also differ in style, tone, and content from the other items in an edition of personal letters, for the public letters invariably lack the sense of being focused on a single recipient; instead they employ the more formalized and abstract rhetoric of public disputation, in which only public provocations are mentioned, though as Richard Ellmann's biography makes clear, there were underlying personal reasons for the public rift between Wilde and Whistler, who had once been good friends.[17] In short, public "letters" really belong among a writer's miscellaneous prose works, along with essays, book reviews, aphorisms, and other short public writings.

Should the text of a "letter" that is actually intended for the public turn up in manuscript, there is seldom any difficulty in distinguishing it as such, for its entire look and rhetoric differ markedly from those of a personal letter.[18] But one of the problems with including public letters in an edition of correspondence is that those that do not survive in manuscript lack all the standard checks applied by scholars to determine the authenticity of other letters, such as the paper and post-marks of a manuscript, biographical details that could be known only to the particular writer, or even personal touches of style with which an editor can verify that a "letter to the editor" was actually written by the supposed author in question and not someone adopting his name or using a similar nom de plume. Such problems led two editors of Percy Bysshe Shelley's *Letters* to attribute to Shelley a letter dated 26 September 1817 to the editor of the *Examiner,* published there on 5 October 1817, that is clearly not by him.[19]

V.
Artful and Artless Correspondence

Besides sorting out the texts clearly prepared for the public from the private and confidential texts, editors can recognize and call attention to the range of variation in the levels of formality or intimacy and other aspects of tone that are to be found even within a particular writer's correspondence. Some letter writers are customarily more formal than others.[20] William Godwin's letters, with the notable exception of his early passionate letters to Mary Wollstonecraft, are almost invariably formal and reticent, just as he is in his laconic journal. Leigh Hunt, conversely, often takes the liberty of appearing more familiar and intimate with his correspondents than the situation warrants, such as when he is asking them for financial help, or otherwise imposing on them. Yet Hunt's tone, like Coleridge's in similar letters to quasi patrons, is governed by the same pride and desire to show his independence that inform the much more formal and reserved tone found in both Godwin's and the Reverend Sidney Smith's letters to those who helped them. Hunt and Coleridge claimed friendship with their patrons as a way of protecting their sense of worth. Godwin, who had never had many friends, sought support on the basis of his philosophical and literary achievements. Many who acknowledged his merits as a thinker and writer heartily disliked him. Hunt, on the other hand, like S. T. Coleridge, was a youngest child who had been coddled within the family; like Coleridge, he followed in the wake of his father, a loyalist Anglican clergyman from Philadelphia who had depended on patronage from the time he fled to England during the American Revolution. Hunt's early poems were patronized by the noble, the rich, and the powerful.[21] Thus, from an early age Hunt's relations with the upper classes had been cordial and deferential in a friendly way, and he repeatedly sought to recover the persona that he had enjoyed in his childhood — that of a beloved dependent, praised for his talents and loved for his sweet temper. These expectations were fulfilled only in his relationship with Shelley, an aristocratic heir with egalitarian ideals who loved to patronize his friends.

Percy Bysshe Shelley carefully tailored his level of intimacy and formality to his purpose of the moment and to his personal situation vis-à-vis his correspondent. Because Shelley believed that Byron was, as he wrote to Peacock in 1816, "poisonously imbued" with "superstitions of rank & wealth & revenge & servility to opinion," Shelley invariably addressed him formally as "My Lord Byron" and kept himself at a safe distance so that Byron could not accuse him of insinuating himself into a status of equality with a peer of the realm.[22] This much we can, with effort, derive from the published texts of their letters. But the manuscripts provide other dimensions of evidence. In his letters to Byron, especially those in which he discusses problems arising between them concerning Claire Clairmont and her daughter Allegra, Shelley's formality can be observed even in his rigid handwriting, in the care of his phrasing, in the relative dearth of cancellations and abbreviations, and even in his use of wax seals that themselves contained messages.[23]

In general, Shelley's early letters are much more spontaneous and personal than his later ones. In his revealing early letters to Hogg, Elizabeth Hitchener, and Godwin, he opened up his soul to the response of those he trusted would sympathize with his hopes and aspirations. As he grew older, having been misunderstood, rebuffed, and even persecuted for his opinions, he became more guarded and circumspect. Like Godwin, Peacock, and Sidney Smith, among others, he developed into what I have elsewhere characterized as an *artful* correspondent.[24] The *artful* style of these men contrasts with the much more *artless* epistolary style of Leigh Hunt, Mary W. Shelley, Hazlitt, and John Keats. Even though all of these writers tailored their tone and the subjects they discussed to the interests and relative status of their individual correspondents, the *artless* writers revealed more fully what was on their minds and expressed the same general opinions to differing correspondents.[25] That many instances of such apparent candor involved considerable artistry, however, can be seen in the examples of Charles Lamb and Byron, who used wit, humor, or exaggeration to maintain apparent consistency of opinion in most of their personal correspondence without offending even those with whom they were quarreling.

VI.
Art in Public and Private Manuscripts

No matter how artful some private letters become, there are still important reasons, I believe, for maintaining the distinction between private and public texts. Even the artful rhetoric of a personal letter depends upon the precise relations between the writer and the recipient(s) in ways that change the meaning when others encounter the same words. When the writings that an author intended to publish are mixed together with personal letters, private journals, marginalia, or rough drafts that may not have been intended even to be read beyond the writer's own intimate circle, readers and critics are apt to misjudge the nature and quality of the writer's overall work. At the literary level, when the collected poetry of Shelley, whose scraps of verse Mary Shelley had so assiduously rescued from his draft notebooks, came to be edited primarily by chronology, rather than by the author's intentions, and the highly polished completed poems (with a few fragments) that he released for publication were juxtaposed with false starts and rejected fragments, the mixture gave readers a less positive picture of Shelley's intelligence, technical skill, and aesthetic judgment, thereby seriously harming his poetic reputation.

Just as letters to periodicals are public documents that, because of a failure to note important differences of intention, are classified with private letters, so some manuscripts that we would at first consider public are actually quite private in nature. The early drafts of many poems and not a few works in prose retain the character of private documents because the author has no intention of showing them to anyone except, perhaps, his or her closest literary advisers. Sometimes they contain passages or notes that he purposely wishes to keep from even those closest friends. The literary drafts in Percy Bysshe Shelley's manuscript notebooks are frequently of this character. Yet editions of Shelley's poetry that are arranged chronologically often make little distinction between his finished, public poetry, published or prepared for the press by him or under his supervision, and his rejected false starts or fragments drawn and heavily edited by others from his rough or interim drafts.

A document prepared by its author for public presentation or for confidential dissemination may require explication when it is taken out of its generative context. For example, a directive to the staff of a governmental agency may need annotation if it is to be published for a wider public, or a poem such as Shelley's *The Mask of Anarchy,* written about a public event in 1819, may require historical annotation when it is republished for American students today. But private and other personal documents by their very nature are never meant to be obvious to anyone except the writer and the recipient, or the very limited circle to whom they are first directed. The very act of publishing them requires that they be edited and annotated in much more fundamental ways than public documents ever should have to be. For example, most private diaries, journals, memoranda, and letters contain private or abbreviated references to people, places, and things that would be obvious to the recipient but would require either expansion or annotation to make them clear to a wider reading public. Keats's friend John Hamilton Reynolds, for example, headed one of his letters to a close friend with a sequence of capital letters: "ASO.S.I.F.S.L." Joanna Richardson, editing this letter, had to annotate the series of initials as the return address of the letter, the insurance office where Reynolds was working at the time: "Amicable Society Office, Serjeants' Inn, Fleet Street, London." In another vein, Charles Lamb's letters of a certain period are filled with allusions to his friends under code names, two of which—"the Professor" and "the Baby"—Edwin W. Marrs, Jr., Lamb's editor, has identified as referring to William and Mary Jane Godwin, respectively.[26]

It is always difficult for one scholar or team of researchers to identify all the odd allusions and references that are necessary to make sense of a personal letter. Sometimes it proves impossible to identify even the date, occasion, and subject, much less the meaning, of a purely private communication, one meant to be cryptic and indecipherable to any but the designated recipient, even given the fullest possible knowledge of the lives of the writer and recipient and the best scholarly research. The evidence for this statement is found in any collective edition of letters, among those letters and notes (often gathered in an appendix of "Letters of Uncertain Date") that begin with a series of queries about the missive's date, place, and/or occasion of writing, occasionally even about the name of the recipient or the writer. Among the Guiccioli-Gamba papers that the Carl H. Pforzheimer Library purchased in 1971 was a folder marked by Teresa Guiccioli "altre donne" ("other women"), which contained twenty-one letters and notes to Byron from various Venetian women seeking to arrange assignations; of these letters, fourteen are anonymous and fifteen are undated. Though we published these private notes in volume 7 of *Shelley and his Circle* after exhaust*ing* if not exhaust*ive* research (we did it perforce in New York, rather than in Venice), for many of them the identity of the writer, the date, and the exact nature of the communication remain, in part, mysterious. Doucet Devin Fischer, who commented on these brief communications in an essay entitled " 'Countesses

and Cobblers' Wives': Byron's Venetian Mistresses," discusses
the meaning of the correspondence as a whole in relation to
Byron's experience in Venice and the probable order and significance of particular letters, as well as the limitations of our
knowledge and the uncertainties that remain.[27] Ultimately, as
those who have looked into volume 7 will know, this correspondence remains not only private but also ephemeral. Perhaps by the time Byron went to Greece, he himself would not
have been able to date or annotate the following note (which
I quote in full in translation):

> I inform you, dear George [*caro Giorgio*], that tomorrow
> at the hour most agreeable to you the Lanetti family, who
> is giving a performance at the Theater of San Moisè, will
> come to see you—let me know what time is suitable, and
> I shall commend them to you—Are you ill? but why do
> I feel worse than you?—
>
> Sunday evening after eight eternal days will I be able
> to see you? Yes.—[28]

Yet Byron would at least have known who the writer was, for
the same woman wrote him at least eight notes in our collection, all anonymous and all undated. By correlating an angry
allusion in another of the eight anonymous notes to "Signor
Petretin(i)" with a mention of the same man in one of Byron's
letters of January 1818, Doucet Fischer speculates that the
woman, apparently a member of the upper classes, may have
been the "Elena da Mosta—a Gentil Donna" of whose health
problems, Byron noted, Petritini had warned him; she "was
clapt—& she has clapt me—to be sure it was *gratis,* the first
Gonorrhea I have not paid for.—"[29] But the identification of
the anonymous writer as Elena da Mosta hangs by this single
thread, being based on just enough mysterious references in
the texts of the six notes to provide a tenuous link—and a
good story, if our primary aim had been to weave a fiction
rather than to establish just what we could know and to admit
the limits of our knowledge. We describe these eight notes by
an "Unidentified Woman to Byron" and date them tentatively
"?January–?March 1818."[30] Even should our speculation be

confirmed that Elena da Mosta was the writer of these very personal notes, unless this identification were accompanied by a great deal of circumstantial information about her life and movements, we would still be in the dark about many of the allusions and references in the eight cryptic texts.

A third reason for maintaining the distinction between public and private texts involves a contrary problem. Just as some private documents are almost impossible to explicate because they lack virtually all of the public contexts that render understanding possible, so in other cases, where a rich history of personal interactions is available to the researcher, private letters may become relatively simple to explicate because they lack several complications that are characteristic of most public documents. To take a well-known case in point, the love letters of Robert Browning and Elizabeth Barrett Barrett before their elopement, together with the correspondence and memoirs of those in their circles, provide such a full context for the fairly simple drama that unfolds within those letters that very little need remain a mystery to the modern student of the couple.[31] We can complicate the story—and biographers do—by speculating on matters that lie outside the relationship between Robert and Elizabeth themselves, such as the feelings between Elizabeth Barrett and her father and between Robert Browning and his mother. But these ghosts hovering over the psyches of the writers do not seriously complicate the issues to any observer who has ever heard of Freud, nor do they affect a straight explication of what is being said in the letters and what all the references and allusions are. This correspondence can, therefore, be read on one level as a clear, straightforward plot, while at the same time its rhetorical structures can be analyzed, or "deconstructed," to arrive at the unstated emotional motivations of the writers.

Thus, though every personal manuscript, like every publication, can involve a degree of rhetorical and aesthetic shaping, scholars and editors of such documents are aware that where there are enough private documents between and about a cohesive group of people, personal documents have fewer such levels of complication. When one analyzes a private exchange between an author and a known recipient, it is often much easier to gauge and delineate the nature of the rhetorical and aesthetic shaping that has taken place and, consequently, to restate the message of the correspondence in terms of the author's original emotions and unstated calculations than is possible with a public or even a corporate document.

VII.
The Complexity of Public Documents

The difference in the complexity of rhetorical analysis depends simply on the few variables in a communication between two known individuals. In construing and then deconstructing a letter passing between Godwin and the mature Shelley, we can see the two men struggling for moral leverage like two sumo wrestlers. In December 1817, after Harriet Shelley's suicide, Shelley and Mary Godwin were finally able to marry. Though Shelley had by this date given Godwin large sums of money to pay his debts, Godwin had managed to refrain from being grateful on the grounds that Shelley had wronged him beyond repair by seducing his only daughter. After the marriage (about which Godwin wrote so complacently to his brother), Godwin continued to ask Shelley for additional money until these importunities, together with the earlier debts he had accumulated and the relatively high cost of living in England, as compared with the Continent, became leading factors in driving Shelley to leave England for Italy. While the Shelley's were abroad, Godwin never ceased bombarding Shelley, both directly and through appeals to Mary, either with demands for more money or with insults for Shelley's failure to fulfill some of his more grandiose promises.

Yet underneath this surface level of moral recrimination about money lay the deeper psychological conflict that Godwin had developed in *Mandeville* (1817), in which within a historical story of the religious hatreds of the seventeenth century he depicts his own hatred of Shelley as his rival for the affections of Mary under the guise of the irrational antipathy of Mandeville for Clifford, who loves and is beloved by Henrietta, Mandeville's only friend. (Their rivalry is confirmed and depicted once again by characters closely resembling Godwin and Shelley who compete for the affection of a surrogate of Mary W. Godwin Shelley in Mary Shelley's novella *Mathilda*.) This hint is all we need to unmask the competition so blatant in the letters, which use moral imperatives drawn from *Enquiry concerning Political Justice* and other early works to play out the games of ethical superiority between father and husband that each hopes will establish his ultimate right to Mary Shelley's undivided affection. Only Shelley's death ended this epistolary duel.

As soon as we turn from these letters and try to analyze either author's public works, even such relatively simple cases as those in *The Esdaile Notebook,* or Shelley's two early Gothic fictions *Zastrozzi* and *St. Irvyne*—to say nothing of the complex historical and psychological matrixes of *Mandeville* itself, in which the historical elements provide an entirely different rationale for all that I have inferred about Godwin's hatred of Shelley—we immediately encounter a deeper level of difficulty altogether. It is not that the rhetoric of the poems or fictions is more sophisticated; some of Shelley's and Godwin's letters, especially in their nuances of tone, are subtler than the rhetoric of Shelley's early poems and novels. But the public works of these men, like those of most fine writers, involve their relations, not with a few other people, but with compounded personal, political, and social concerns, as they drew upon the full range of their cultural knowledge and personal experience in their responses to historical and contemporary public events. Some poems in *The Esdaile Notebook* describe moods and events that Shelley may have experienced just before he wrote them, but other poems—such as the ones on the Battle of Austerlitz ("To the Emperors of Russia & Austria"), the Mexican revolt against Spain ("To the Republicans of North America"), and his "Fragment . . . suggested by the bombardment of Copenhagen"—describe or react to events that he knew only from his reading or from stories told to him by friends.[32] Into this mix we must add

Shelley's attempts to master various literary conventions, including verse forms, traditional figures of speech, and traditional thematic concerns. Finally, there remains the question of Shelley's relations with the audiences he envisioned for his writing. The scope and nature of his intended audience for a particular work may become clear from Shelley's comments in his letters, from a note or preface, or from a contemporary remark by a friend about his intentions. But sometimes even a complete archaeological analysis of one of these early poems leaves us only with shards and fragments that provide an approximate date within a range of two or three years, a possible occasion, and a generalized audience that might include any readers he could find, though possibly imagined as his peers in intelligence and education.

Failure to distinguish between public and private documents has produced much of the misunderstanding and wasted effort in recent literary criticism. Whereas John Freeman's analysis of Shelley's letters to his father actually unveils the emotions beneath the language of those letters in a way that can win the assent of most readers approaching those texts, even though they may look at the situation from a variety of psychological perspectives,[33] much of the deconstructive criticism of Shelley's poetry—including readings by such masters of the game as Paul de Man and J. Hillis Miller[34]—is so palpably fragmentary and partial that except insofar as it draws its ideas from scholar-critics who have utilized conventional methods of research, it not only fails to advance the discussion but, in the view of the most knowledgeable critics, seems to trivialize the great poems discussed. Frequently, the deconstructive readings point out less obvious resonances and less likely potential meanings of some of the figures of speech in the poems; but the final significance of even these selected tropes depends upon a larger framework of meanings that can be established only through the study of Shelley's biography and intellectual development, his other writings (especially those in which parallel figures of speech and rhetorical structures appear), his literary sources, the generic and metrical traditions within which he wrote particular poems, the historical occasions of his writing, and the overall structural and thematic patterning of the poems in which these tropes appear.

For some time it has been apparent that the general method of deconstructive criticism was one valid way of approaching a text and that every text is, indeed, made up of choices and decisions that force the writer to abandon or deemphasize some aspects of his or her feelings, thought, and artistry in order to display and shape other aspects. It follows, then, that every text contains some words but not others, in certain arrangements rather than other possible ones, with the words framed, for instance, not as a statement but as a question: "If winter come, can spring be far behind?" Such choices thus provide both "presences," things actually written, and "absences," words and structures that clarify the choices that were made by the fact that these alternative possibilities were *not* chosen to appear in the text. But the range of absences is nearly infinite, and to explicate the meaning of a passage by fixing on one particular alternative meaning of multivalent phrases or to suggest one of a plethora of unarticulated thoughts as the unstated or repressed meaning of the poem is as fallacious as to deny that the author had choices to make in the first place.

Several things that Paul de Man says about Shelley in "Shelley Disfigured," his essay about "The Triumph of Life," are both true and important (though most of the factual matters and intertextual allusions had been noted earlier).[35] Why, then, does de Man's reading fail to confront the basic problems of "The Triumph" or to account for its effects on sensitive readers of poetry? Quite apart from the critic's ideological commitment to finding in all texts a loss of belief and a disintegration of values (and de Man's hidden motivations for that ideology may be clearer now than in 1979, when he published "Shelley Disfigured"), the tools of rhetorical analysis that de Man employs in the essay are simply inadequate for his task.

First, the analysis of syntax and figures of speech has no capacity to reach beyond the text into the existential issues of despair that de Man purports to analyze, which must be pursued behind the words into the psyche of the poet—a human being like us—insofar as that is revealed by the totality of all his writings (public and private), accounts of his actions and conversations, and the surviving analytical comments of all his friends and acquaintances. Materials are now available to explore his biographical situations and his reactions to them in great detail, and such analysis enables us to realize both the depths and the complexities of Shelley's despair, which de Man merely accepts as a given, offering a sketch of the situation that is a simplified version of the one offered by those of us who had previously explored it. But even if Shelley had not felt desperate in 1822 because of his lack of poetic recognition and influence—even if he had, instead, been a successful diplomat and court poet, praised by rulers and the populace alike—he might still have used the very same imagery to express some timeless truths about the human condition, as did Petrarch when he wrote his *Trionfi* (ca. 1351–74) in the fullness of his fame and honor. Petrarch's *Trionfi* was paralleled and was probably modeled on both Boccaccio's *L'Amorosa visione* (1342–43) and the terza rima predecessor of both works, Dante's *Commedia,* which, in turn, was shaped by a rich literary and historical tradition. Shelley was also influenced directly by Dante, by Milton (both *Comus* and *Paradise Lost* are clearly evoked in "The Triumph of Life"), by Rousseau's *Confessions* and *Julie* (which Shelley took to be an idealized and symbolic representation of Rousseau's quest for love, much as *Epipsychidion* represented his own), by such contemporary poets as Wordsworth, Byron, and Goethe, and by the imagery and structure of Shelley's own earlier completed major poems, all of which not only were written in far different moods but reverse the negative implications of the same imagery that de Man finds so self-defeating. The chariot of Life, for example, which Shelley drew from Ezekiel by way of Milton's "chariot of Paternal Deitie" and a beautifully serene picture of the Car of the Church in Dante's *Purgatorio,* was used by him in act 4 of *Prometheus Unbound* to achieve an entirely different effect of power and serenity.[36]

De Man, from his reading of previous scholarship, was perfectly aware of these intertextual complexities, and yet, trapped by his methodology, he selected only a few possible meanings that would support his viewpoint as the ones Shelley must have suppressed. De Man's criticism starved on a macrobiotic diet while a harvest feast was on the table. To explore the alternatives that Shelley suppressed in "The Triumph of Life," one would have to lay out the entire, undifferentiated veil of thought against which the particular poem is silhouetted; as Shelley himself figures the dilemma of the poet and of humanity in "Hymn to Intellectual Beauty," one would have to define that which "to human thought [is] nourishment, / Like darkness to a dying flame." Instead, de Man chooses to limit Shelley's choices of meaning to two possibilities—one totally congruent with Shelley's other, completed, public poems, the other congruent only with de Man's thematic reading of every other romantic poem he ever explicated. Somehow, according to de Man's reading, "The Triumph" actually meant, not what Shelley had previously asserted, but what de Man had previously asserted.

Last, but certainly not least in the context of this discussion, de Man ignored entirely the most obvious complicating factor of "The Triumph of Life": the sole authority for the poem (apart from its first twenty lines) is a fragmentary rough draft that Shelley not only had kept from the public but apparently had not shown even to his wife or his most confidential friends, who discovered it after his death.[37] What now passes for a public poem was wrested from the inchoate manuscript by editors, beginning with the heroic effort of Mary W. Shelley before 1824. The proper way to explicate "The Triumph," I am now convinced, is the way he left it, in all its incompleteness and confusion. The poem cannot be deconstructed, because Shelley did not live long enough to decide what he would suppress or exile from the poem and what he would include. And if de Man's method could not tame even the domesticated cat of those edited versions, how could he claim to have confronted the tiger in the jungle of false starts, abrupt turns, and half-canceled lines that must be included to continue the terza rima? One reason the deconstructionists analyze "The Triumph of Life" rather than *The Witch of Atlas, Adonais, Hellas,* or Shelley's other late completed poems is that these critics feel free to pick and choose among the variants for evidence to support their prefabricated conception of its meaning. They fail to acknowledge that before the author himself has chosen among the infinite possibilities to complete the plot and symbolic patterns—before he has constructed the poem—there is nothing to deconstruct.

This uncompleted manuscript, not yet coherent enough for the poet to share with his confidential advisers, was a private aide-mémoire, the farthest thing from a public communication. Had Shelley lived to copy fair more than the first twenty lines and had he shared these with Mary Shelley or others, that new manuscript would have been a *confidential* one that, with the aid of revelations from those whom Shelley consulted, we might begin to discuss as critics analyze uncompleted sculptures or buildings from plans and models. But since Shelley drowned before confiding in anyone about the poem, the draft was reduced, in effect, to a nonentity, though an intriguing one.[38] The *private* manuscript of "The Triumph of Life" has now the same status as a bowl containing some of the ingredients of a cake. Shelley had chosen a rhyme scheme, a level of diction, a tone, protagonists, and some basic metaphors; lacking are the development of the plot, the denouement, and (therefore) the overall structure and meaning of the work. The flour, sugar, baking powder, and eggs are mixed, but the flavor has not been added. Will it be a chocolate cake, a spice cake, or a white cake? What has the baker produced before? What stock of flavors are available to him?

As this is not the place to undertake a complete reading of "The Triumph of Life" on the scale that is required, I also must leave my thought unfinished. But the general direction of my message is already clearer than is Shelley's in his enigmatic final fragment. And readers who desire further enlightenment can sample other cakes by this baker, as well as other poems by Shelley.

CHAPTER FOUR

PRIVATE AND PUBLIC MANUSCRIPTS:

AUTHORIAL INTENTION AND

READER RESPONSE

❖

I.
Confidential Manuscripts and Their Audience

As we have seen, the primary factor that categorizes a manuscript as *private, confidential,* or *public* is not its degree of artfulness or the level of personal intimacy between the writer and its readers but the nature and extent of the writer's intended audience. A manuscript is *private* if its author intended it to be read only by one person or a specific small group of people whose identity he knew in advance; *confidential* if it was intended for a predefined but larger audience who may— or may not—be personally known to or interested in the author; and *public* only if it was written to be published or circulated for perusal by a widespread, unspecified audience, including such abstractions as the nation, the reading public, and posterity.[1]

The degree of interest for readers that *any* type of manuscript material commands depends, obviously, on the expectations and the purposes of the audience that encounters it. I can illustrate the problem of expectations from an account of the discovery in 1953 of the key to the Linear B syllabary script and the deciphering of the clay tablets from Pylos and

Cnossos—voluminous writings from the Achaean civilization of the thirteenth to the fifteenth century B.C.E.:

> Before decipherment, many dreams were woven around the contents of the tablets: they were thought to contain religious and literary texts, possibly a primitive Iliad or Odyssey. These hopes proved idle. The tablets were solely administrative documents, lists and inventories. Their attention to detail was particularly remarkable; they contained a record of the weight of bronze distributed to manufacture 500,000 arrow heads or 2,300 swords, as well as the numbers of smiths active in every village, the number of pigs a district must provide, the quantity of corn destined to sow the different categories of soil, the number of wheels stored in the magazines at the palace of Cnossos, the ration of corn and figs allotted to the thirty-seven serving women at the baths of Pylos. The most personal details did not escape the curiosity of the administration: a certain Pesero had a wife and two children; another man had two slaves, a man and a woman; in one place there were two chariots, one of which was out of use. . . .
>
> The Achaean monarchies thus appear to have been supported by a powerful and omniscient bureaucracy, like the ones in the Middle East. . . . None of this appears in Homer, where the kings were solely war chiefs, only notable for their wealth and warlike exploits. In actual fact, they headed a complex and pettifogging administration, which found its fundamental tool in the invention of writing.[2]

For anthropologists, social historians, and linguists such an archive of tax records might be invaluable, but for the humanistic scholar or historian of ideas this kind of *confidential* bureaucratic record offers a less satisfying experience. In this and in many other instances, the gap between our intellectual expectations and the contents of corporate governmental records has to do with the distinction between *confidential* and *public* documents.

A confidential manuscript is intended by its author to inform or direct a group of colleagues in the performance of some activity connected with the purpose for which the confidential group was formed. The information on the Achaean tablets was obviously used by, among others, the tax assessors of the day to make sure that the state received its share of the wealth. The biblical epistles of St. Paul—and those by other authors assuming his name and authority—were also confidential documents, attempts by the apostle to teach and strengthen the faith of various young communities of Christians, most of which Paul himself had founded. Those who were in the faith, especially those who were trying to define its significance for their own lives, found these letters very valuable. They might also have found an unintended audience in the Roman authorities leading the persecution of Christians under Diocletian, who might have read them as primary evidence of the mind-set and subversive doctrines of their quarry. For these epistles to gain value as *public* documents, however, the society at large had to take an interest in the historical and doctrinal dimensions of Christianity.

If we were today handed a collection of the autograph epistles by a leading living proselytizer on behalf of Sun Myung Moon and his Unification Church, or by a leading light in the Hare Krishna sect, we might well (after a phone call to Sotheby's and Christie's to make sure that they lacked commercial value) throw them out without reading them through. Such confidential missives to fellow believers would embody mutual expectations on the part of the writers and their intended readers that would confine their comprehensibility to the initiated, and only outsiders who studied the faith as students of comparative religion or psychology might be tempted to read the documents with sufficient interest and aesthetic distance to determine whether they, like Paul's epistles, happened to exhibit literary merit.

Similar conditions govern other kinds of *confidential* documents. Internal governmental and business reports meant to be read within a department or division are apt to be boring, if not totally unintelligible, to anyone not directly affected by the information and the decisions they transmit. For such documents to gain widespread interest, they must be deciphered, and their significance analyzed for the public. As I mentioned above, many government and business scandals are exposed by the publication of such confidential memos and documents. But even in these instances, the significance of the documents becomes clear to the reading public only after detailed explication either by members of the confidential group to which they were directed or by knowledgeable investigators who have studied the agency, corporation, or discipline for which the missives were written.

Since both *personal* letters and manuscripts and *confidential* epistles, memos, and documents are directed at specific, limited audiences, their authors seldom expend any effort to reach out to other potential readers. Such documents as love letters and memos from bosses to their workers, urging greater production or total secrecy, may attempt to persuade. But even this rhetoric usually need not include any effort to bridge a perceived gap between the writer and the intended reader(s), for the limits of the audience have already been defined by a preestablished communality between the writer and those to whom such a memo is sent. A self-conscious effort to define and distinguish the "self" or "us" from "the other" or "them" and to reach across that gap may, therefore, differentiate *public* documents from other kinds of documents. This would explain why public documents depend so heavily on formal conventions, such as genre, prosody, and intertextual allusion: they represent attempts to establish a common ground between writer and a diverse group of potential readers.

II.

Three Types of Travel Diary

Let me illustrate the differences between the various types of manuscripts by examining briefly three travel notebooks kept by members of the Shelley circle—first, a *private journal* and account book kept by Edward John Trelawny; second, a *con-*

fidential diary kept by Maria Gisborne during her trip from Italy to England from May to September 1820 that was meant to be shown to the Shelleys upon the Gisbornes' return to Italy; and third, a *public travel diary* kept by Edward Ellerker Williams, the half-pay army lieutenant who drowned with Shelley.

Trelawny's private journal, a version of which opens volume 8 of *Shelley and his Circle*,[3] has its front pastedown and both sides of the conjugate first leaf filled with miscellaneous notations—financial calculations, names, dates, a sketch of three peasant women, a quotation from a poem, a note from a travel book, and the draft of more than a dozen lines of apparently original poetry running in different directions on the three pages. Three concluding lines of the poetic draft appear at the top of folio 2 recto, the remainder of which contains the beginning of a four-page list of Trelawny's books. This book list, carefully and neatly written within hand-ruled grids, records titles, authors, and the number of volumes of each entry. The careful form suggests that this part of the notebook was intended to fulfill a *quasi-public* purpose, and we surmise that Trelawny listed those books that he left in the care of his landlord in Switzerland when he returned to England after learning in September 1820 of his father's death, with the idea that he could use the list to make sure that his books were intact when he returned. Most of the rest of the notebook, insofar as it survives, lists daily payments for furniture, food, fuel, and other housekeeping expenses incurred when Trelawny was in Italy from "December 6, 1821, through March 8, 1822—over a month at Genoa and Trelawny's first month and a half at Pisa" with the Shelley-Byron circle (*Shelley and his Circle*, 8:703). This part of the notebook is a *private* document, consisting of jotted records, on Sunday, 6 January, for example, listing the prices Trelawny paid for "Wood," "Meat," "Minestra," "Bread," "Salt," "Vinegar," and "Butter Salad & Milk" (8:657). These notes may be of interest only to economic and social historians who want to know how well the younger brother of an English baronet could live in Italy in the 1820s on an income of three hundred pounds per year and to students of Shelley and Byron, who, by comparing these lists with another diary kept simultaneously by Edward Ellerker Williams, may learn more about the interactions of the Pisan circle centered on Byron and Shelley early in 1822. But much of the record of Trelawny's daily expenses remains uncommunicative. There is no indication that he moved from Genoa to Pisa while he was keeping this daily record. We know what he expended on food and wood and rushes for the floor, but we do not know how much "Wood" (presumably firewood) he bought for 50 paoli (or pauls) on the sixth of January, or what kind of "Meat" he bought, or how it was cooked or served. Some of the entries are undated, and dates for these must be conjectured; the private meaning of certain words can be guessed at but not verified.

Publishing *private* documents of this sort—the proverbial laundry lists—always entails a risk, because reviewers are seldom as impressed by what they reveal as is the scholar who takes up the challenge of trying to explicate them. Were *Shelley and his Circle* not the comprehensive project it is, or were more known from other sources about Trelawny's life between his divorce in 1817 and his arrival at Pisa in 1822, we might have been content to publish a few bits of information from the notebook, along with the semipublic book list, and leave the rest of the document for future gleaners. But Trelawny had stretched the truth so much in his retrospective autobiographical accounts that it seemed important to lay out all of the contemporary documentary evidence as a useful check on his veracity. As it was, by undertaking the difficult task of editing the entire manuscript for *Shelley and his Circle,* William St. Clair was able to write a useful essay that supplements and corrects his account of the same period in his biography *Trelawny: The Incurable Romancer.*[4]

The journal kept by Maria Gisborne during her trip to England is a *confidential* one, as we know from Mary Shelley's correspondence with her about it, or as one might realize from the nature of its revelations.[5] Before marrying John Gisborne and moving to Italy, Maria James Reveley had not only cared for the infant Mary Shelley in 1797, after the death of Mary

Wollstonecraft Godwin, but received a proposal of marriage from William Godwin in 1799, after the sudden death of her first husband Willey Reveley. Mary Godwin Shelley, desiring news of her father and others in London, asked Maria Gisborne to keep a journal during the Gisbornes' trip to England in the summer of 1820 for Mary to read when the Gisbornes returned to Italy. In this journal, Mrs. Gisborne refers to Mary Shelley in ways that make clear that it was meant for her perusal. Because Maria Gisborne's intention was to keep the journal *confidential* but not *private,* its meaning is perfectly comprehensible at first reading to anyone immersed in the study of the Shelleys, whose friends are frequently mentioned in it. (The only names needing annotation for those conversant with the Shelleys and their circle are those of a few relatives of the Gisbornes.) While there are several incidental anecdotes about the journey to and from England such as might appear in a published travel book, most of the material would at that time have interested only someone with a direct interest in the Godwin and Shelley circles, though as the following two consecutive entries, the first that were written in London, suggest, the fame of those in the circles has now made parts of this journal a viable public record.

Sunday, June 11. London.—We called yesterday upon Mr. Godwin, I believe I made a very bad figure in this first interview; I could say nothing but silly things. He appeared very glad to see me, I should rather say elated. We were introduced to Mrs. Godwin, she was suffering from so great an hysterical agitation that she could scarcely speak. I think her rather pretty, but her physiognomy is determinedly bad. Mr. Godwin is become much more corpulent; I remember him very thin, even with a certain degree of sharpness of feature, which is now entirely lost.

Friday, June 23. Yesterday evening we drank tea at Mr. Hunts; we found him ill, as he had been attacked with a bilious fever, soon after we last saw him and was not yet recovered. His nephew was with him; he appears grave, and very attentive to his uncle, listening to all his words, in silence. Mr. Keats was introduced to us the same evening; he had lately been ill also, and spoke but little; the Endymion was not mentioned, this person might not be its author; but on observing his countenance and his eyes I persuaded myself that he was the very person. We talked of music, and of Italian and english singing; I mentioned that Farinelli had the art of taking breath imperceptibly, while he continued to hold one single note, alternately swelling out and diminishing the power of his voice like the waves. Keats observed that this must in some degree be painful to the hearer, as when a diver descends into the hidden depths of the sea you feel an apprehension lest he may never rise again. These may not be his exact words as he spoke in a low tone.[6]

Before Edward and Jane Williams had met Trelawny and long before they went to Pisa to meet Shelley, Edward had written a document that, though he entitled it "Private Journal," was clearly intended as a *public* document, probably written with a view to publication. This judgment derives from the appearance of the document itself, from its reticent tone and the exclusively *public* matter it contains, from its affinity to the genre of the travel books of the period (a form less conventionally precise than the epic or sonnet, yet recognizable by those who have read a number of them), and from discrepancies between its account of Edward Williams's journey from England and through France to Switzerland and Williams's account of the same events in a more famous, *really private* journal that he kept from 1821 until he drowned with Shelley in July 1822.

The "Private Journal" of 1819 begins thus: "After having shaken a few dear friends by the hand I quitted London about half past 3 o'clock on the aft^n of Friday the 28th May 1819 with my friend Cox as Compagnon$ du Voyage, and arrived at Brighton at ten the same night, having traveled *Post* from Town. — "[7] There is nothing here that is private — no expression of emotion, no first names of the "few dear friends" or even of "Cox"; to call the latter both "my friend" and "Compagnon du Voyage" marks the journal as public, since if the writer were keeping the journal for his own recollection, he would be perfectly aware of their relationship and would instead have recorded such matters as his private reasons for going abroad, or his feelings about doing so. Within the entries for the next few days, we find many sentences that are clearly designed to aid the traveling public but have little or nothing to do with private journal memoranda. For example, in the next entry, after describing the crossing of the channel in rough seas, Williams writes: "It may, perhaps, be as well to remark that should ladies be inclined to embark at Brighton, it is strongly recommended that a *Schooner* rather than a *Cutter* should be selected, the motion of the last being considerably increased by the weight of the boom, causing a most unpleasant see-saw pitching—" As I wrote of this document in *Shelley and his Circle,* in "this self-styled 'Private Journal,'"

we find . . . nothing private, but rather the staple stuff of the travel books popular during the period. Comments on crossing the channel, information on the passport and customs check, and remarks about the hotel at Dieppe . . . would have been appropriate, perhaps, for either private reminiscence or public perusal. But it is difficult to imagine an ordinary tourist, writing simply to record the highlights of his trip to aid his own memory in later years, giving the history of the cathedral of Rouen as Williams does . . . or recording that the belfry of the cathedral contained "the largest bell in Europe if we except that of Moscow."[8]

III.
Communication in Private and Public Discourse

In private, confidential, and public discourse alike, the reader must examine such semimechanical elements as miswritten words, muddled syntax, and ambiguous phraseology to determine what meaning the writer intended to convey. Personal letters, like other forms of communication, often require rhetorical analysis to determine the writer's tone and the extent to which the writer was trying to persuade or manipulate the recipient. Sometimes the most crucial finding of such close analysis of private correspondence is that the writer is being ironic, or is employing another protective disguise to hide his or her real feelings. In *Shelley and his Circle,* Kenneth Neill Cameron and I have analyzed many of Shelley's letters to his college friend Thomas Jefferson Hogg and to Lord Byron, while John Freeman has similarly scrutinized Shelley's letters to his father.[9] Our conclusions are far from startling: there are strong rhetorical undercurrents in these letters that modify the surface messages they seem to convey. Such analysis of the rhetorical structures and devices that were employed by a rather repressed young man to disguise and yet reveal his feelings toward his father and friends ought to warn biographers and critics to break the easy habit of trying to prove a point by quoting passages from a poet's private letters out of their relational contexts. That can no more be done safely than one can quote a speech of a character in one of Shakespeare's dramas and attribute the sentiment without qualification to Shakespeare himself. The "feelings" Shelley expresses to one friend may contradict those he confides to another, and biographers or critics must take into account both Shelley's long-term relationship with his correspondent and the particular situation in which he wrote the letter being cited before knowing what weight they can give a passage quoted outside its native context.

As I suggested above, most *public* documents also involve another dimension of intentionality that transcends the merely syntactical and rhetorical levels. At the rhetorical level, the author of an argumentative treatise such as Shelley's *A Defence of Poetry* may be trying to persuade his friend Thomas Love Peacock and others in British society in 1821 that the cultivation of poetry is a nobler and more socially beneficial activity than is merely fulfilling a pragmatic role, such as Peacock's work at the East India Company. But underlying that rhetorical or practical intention was Shelley's deeper psychological need to save himself from despair by justifying his own life choices, and when we probe still deeper, we find that a more profound and more nearly intrinsic intentionality had led Shelley to make those life choices in the first place: to forgo his patrimony as the pampered son of a wealthy landowner and try to change the society and the world for the better, first by political pamphleteering and direct political action and only later by creating in poetry "beautiful idealisms of moral excellence."

Furthermore, behind Shelley's dedication to these ideals there was a tradition that includes artists and critics from the ancient Greeks and Romans down through Dante, Montaigne, Sir Philip Sidney, Spenser, Shakespeare, Milton, Pope, Chatterton, Cowper, and Burns and also includes the early publications of Wordsworth, Coleridge, and other older contemporaries that had helped inspire Shelley's early choices. Thus, to analyze the intentions of Shelley's essay on poetry solely in terms of his friendly rivalry with Peacock may elucidate the biographical situation of the months during which the essay was written, but it will be only peripherally true to the total intentionality of the essay. This Mary W. Shelley must have felt in 1840, when she first published it, for she discarded the specific allusions to "The Four Ages of Poetry," Peacock's by then forgotten essay of twenty years earlier, in order to emphasize the essay's more fundamental *public* concerns. She reasoned that Shelley wanted to say those particular things about literature and that Peacock's essay in the first (and, as it happened, the only) issue of *Ollier's Literary Miscellany* had merely provided him with a pretext and (he thought) a medium in which to publish it.

To take another example, Coleridge several times revised "The Rime of the Ancient Mariner" between the time of its first publication in *Lyrical Ballads* and the publication of the final version that had his attention in his *Poetical Works* of 1834. In *Lyrical Ballads,* both the title and text of the poem were burdened with pseudoarchaic spellings and diction that Coleridge clearly employed to distance it in time and give added universality to a poem that proves, upon analysis, to be very personally revealing. Later he replaced the archaic diction with the gloss, which performs the same function. The rhetorical levels of the "Ancient Mariner" are so complex that dozens of literary scholar-critics and hundreds of teachers have found useful employment in attempting to unravel them and tracing the individual strands of *personal* psychology, *corporate* religious thought and feeling, and *public* philosophy and artistry. Yet the work seems inexhaustible, because its integration is much more complex and profound than can be encompassed in paraphrastic rhetorical or thematic analyses.

The greater power of *public* texts and other objects of aesthetic distinction lies in the greater universality they achieve by involving themselves with conventions and even words that they adopt from others. Since they are written as parables or tropes drawn from a *public*, traditional, and psychologically valid store of mythic figures, they can communicate with diverse readers according to their individual experiences. Whereas a *private* document depends upon the shared experience of the writer and one or a few pretargeted readers, and whereas *confidential*, corporate documents depend upon a universe of discourse shared by members of a limited community, the *public* document will transcend both the idols of the cave and those of the tribe, reaching toward more universal symbols and structures familiar to readers who participate in a broad cultural heritage.

IV.
*Tact and the Publication of
Private Documents*

As scholars, we participate in the transformation of *private* or *confidential* documents into *public* ones. Because my colleagues and I edit the papers of authors long dead, we seldom encounter difficulty in obtaining permission to publish them or cases where the personal feelings of living relatives are involved in the materials we publish. Our chief problems relate to strategies for editing the manuscripts so that they become accessible to a larger readership than the few dedicated scholars who wish to know *everything* about Shelley, Byron, and their friends and relations. A large number of the documents that have appeared in volumes 7 and 8 of *Shelley and his Circle* and that will appear in subsequent volumes are papers that the Pforzheimer Library purchased privately in 1971 and in subsequent public and private sales.[10] The documents, which had been saved or collected by Countess Teresa Guiccioli, include most of her letters to Byron, as well as letters written to Byron by women with whom he was earlier involved at Venice, together with letters written to Teresa Guiccioli by Percy and Mary Shelley, Thomas Moore, and other correspondents, mostly about the countess's life with Byron; there are also several accounts by her of that liaison, some in Italian and some in French. In addition there are personal and family papers involving her separation from Count Alessandro Guiccioli, as well as papers by and about her brother Count Pietro Gamba, who went to Greece with Byron and, after escorting Byron's body to England and writing a book about Byron in Greece, himself went back to die in the war for Greek independence. Finally, there are many books about Byron's life and poetry once owned by Teresa Guiccioli, many of which contain her annotations.

In chapter 3, I illustrated some problems of understanding *private* correspondence by reference to a letter from an anonymous Venetian woman to Byron. Here I shall take a more complex example, drawn from the very rich vein of some fifty substantial letters that Teresa Guiccioli wrote to Byron from Filetto, her father's villa near Ravenna, between July 1820, when she separated from her husband, and November of the same year. (Most of these will appear in volume 9 of *Shelley and his Circle*.) In a postscript to her letter of 3 August 1820, Teresa wrote, "Today my cousins came here." This seemed at first to offer no special problems — except the question of which cousins may have been paying a visit to Filetto at this time — until my colleague Daniela Noè called to my attention a more expansive parallel allusion in a later letter in this series. A

reading of historical accounts of the time for another commentary raised yet a third possibility, and not being the person
to whom this very private reference was directed, I was forced
to lay out the evidence thus:

> We are unable to identify which cousins—never named—
> Teresa [Guiccioli] alludes to in the postscript as having
> arrived at Filetto. But "Cousins" seems likely to be a
> coded reference. One possible meaning of the allusion
> would involve the Carbonari. According to one account
> of the origins of the movement "in the French department
> of the Jura" (near Switzerland), it was "there called Cou-
> sinship, or Good Cousinship *(Le Bon Cousinage)*" and
> the Carbonari in the Kingdom of Naples apparently also
> called each other "Good Cousins." The presence at Filetto
> of Carbonari from Ravenna or, possibly, from other cities
> might well have deterred Byron's visit, because not only
> were the Gambas anxious to maintain the illusion that
> Teresa was living a chaste life under her father's protection
> (as the Pope's decree provided), but also because if the
> spies of Count Guiccioli had shadowed Byron to Filetto
> and discovered a meeting of Carbonari leaders there, they
> might have exposed that to the authorities.
>
> A second possible coded meaning of the visit of the
> "cousins" may be that Teresa desires Byron to postpone
> his visit because her menstrual period has just begun and
> she wishes to see him after it has finished. This interpre-
> tation depends upon a lengthier allusion in Teresa's letter
> to Byron of 26 October 1820.

> > Come, my Happiness, I desire you with an extreme
> > impatience—but shall I deceive you? It is not pos-
> > sible—yesterday there was an enormous flood here—
> > well then?—I had a lovely elegant thought, my Pet,
> > that is gone—so I shall tell you simply—my Cousins
> > are here with me! Telling you costs me dearly because
> > I fear that it |will delay your coming—remember that
> > they are not staying more than three days, my Pet.—

The entire context here, as well as the language in which Teresa says that "my Cousins are here with me!" rather than that *our* Cousins (or "Good Cousins") are visiting *us* or staying at Filetto, suggests to us that the references to "Cousins" in [three of Teresa Guiccioli's letters to Byron] probably relate, not to revolutionary councils, but to Countess Guiccioli's menstrual cycles. Such cryptic or coded references and allusions as may be found in any strictly private correspondence ultimately defy explication beyond all doubt.[11]

In cases involving authors who are still living or recently deceased, there are often obstacles to such translation of manuscripts from *private* to *public*. The lawsuit in the United States in which the reclusive J. D. Salinger successfully prevented his letters from being quoted or closely paraphrased in a biography of him and the recent uproar about the destruction of peripheral private manuscripts of members of James Joyce's family have highlighted what biographical writers are once again beginning to realize is a complicated question that pits a legitimate right to privacy of living individuals against a legitimate search for the truth about the creation and the creators of important public documents.[12]

The late Richard Ellmann obviously faced a challenge of this kind when he published the more-than-intimate love letters written by James Joyce to Nora Barnacle Joyce in 1909 and 1913, in which Joyce expatiates on his sexual desires and his occasionally eccentric sexual tastes. That these are not letters that even Joyce at his most exhibitionist intended for publication seems clear from his comments within them about their private nature. In his preface to *Selected Letters of James Joyce* (1975), Ellmann shows his awareness of the problems involved, for after alluding to the limited censorship of these letters in the earlier edition of Joyce's *Letters*, he writes:

This correspondence commands respect for its intensity and candour, and for its fulfilment of Joyce's avowed determination to express his whole mind. I hope that readers will not only countenance it but recognize its value as an extreme of Joyce's, and perhaps of human, utterance. The part these letters played in his life is set forth in the Introduction to this volume. . . . They had their effect upon the sexual imagery of his books, where, however, their blunt ardour was made more subtle.[13]

Later in his introduction, Ellmann also mentions that although Joyce exhibits little or no humor in these very private letters to Nora (or in those that survive from another, similar series he wrote to Martha Fleischmann in Zurich in 1918–19), when he later came to make use of these emotional experiences in *Ulysses* and *Finnegan's Wake* he "recognized the implicit comedy."

These intimate letters make painful reading, not, I submit, because Joyce's sexuality shocks us, but because we feel ashamed of our own prurient eavesdropping on so private and intimate a conversation. Like Hazlitt's unrevised letters to Peter George Patmore about his ill-fated passion for his landlord's young daughter Sarah Walker, the documents may just be too intensely personal and private to bear the light of general publication. As Ellmann suggests, those who know Joyce's life and works as well as he did may be able to appreciate the letters as part of their larger story of human striving and artistic achievement, just as devotees of Hazlitt can read with understanding his *private* letters to Peter George Patmore describing the course of his love for Sarah Walker. But those of us capable of empathizing with Hazlitt constitute, in a sense, a confidential circle of close friends across time—a group of Peter George Patmores whose chief pain in reading these letters comes from the empathy we feel for Hazlitt's mental anguish, however misdirected. The "strangers" in the public may find these letters meaningful only when they are set in the artistic public frame of the semifictionalized *Liber Amoris,* which, like Joyce's *Ulysses,* was intended for, and hence shaped to be acceptable to, the reading public.[14]

If there were a way for Joyce's heirs to grant the right to read his very *private* letters only to those who had spent ten years or so mastering the author's *public* writings and biography, those happy few could place the revelations of the letters within contexts of humane appreciation of the nature and dilemma of James and Nora Joyce without feeling that the decorum of communication had been violated. But if such a regimen were required of would-be readers, they would no longer constitute a reading *public,* but a *confidential* group such as can—at some distance in time—be trusted to read any *private* correspondence. Joyce's intimate letters, however, were published not in a scholarly edition that would be primarily read by students of his fiction but in the most widely circulated selection of his letters; these previously restricted letters were, moreover, advertised on the dust jacket as the special feature of the edition, with their dates given so that anyone interested in only the salacious parts could skip the rest of the letters. One can well imagine schoolboys passing around a well-marked copy of Joyce's *Selected Letters,* just as Byron and his friends at Harrow thumbed the appendix in their text of the Latin erotic poets to which all the most salacious passages had been exiled.

Since Ellmann's death, his own confidential correspondence of the recent past with various Joyce scholars and with the representatives of the Joyce estate concerning Hans Walter Gabler's synoptic edition of *Ulysses* has been rifled by Charles Rossman, and parts of it have been quoted in the *New York Review of Books,* thus turning Ellmann posthumously into a gossip about his colleagues in a way that a scholar of his accomplishments and standing might well deplore.[15] I do not think that I am alone in believing that the long-term cause of scholarship would be better served if all of us who engage in the search for truth could also remind ourselves of the need for tact and humanity in deciding whether, when, and under what conditions to publish *private* and *confidential* documents. For if I were the heir to an archive of a major writer who had written letters like those that James Joyce wrote to Nora Joyce, I might well decide to destroy parts of that record rather than have it disseminated without discretion. After seeing the abuse of confidentiality that resulted from the opening of Ellmann's papers for early publication, other scholars and their heirs who donate or sell archives to institutions may well decide to specify that none of the private correspondence be made available to others for a period of years.

I certainly do not advocate the suppression or withholding of any *public* document, or even of *confidential* documents that relate to governmental affairs or public policy and welfare. But discretion and tact in the use of purely *private* correspondence should be a sine qua non of all humanistic scholarship. A love of truth is a great virtue, but like other good things, it sometimes conflicts with other moral rights. If scholars are given access to unpublished documents and thereby can avoid making erroneous statements in their biographical studies, they can call these papers to the attention of other biographers in footnotes, so that their sources and authority will be clear without the publication of all these documents at a time or place that may embarrass or hurt the children or other intimates of the person whose life is being analyzed. Perhaps we humanistic scholars ought to make more efforts to distinguish ourselves from purely objective scientists, sensationalist journalists, and main-chance careerists by our capacity to sympathize with the all-too-human secrets of the men and women to whom we devote our working lives and with the feelings of the children and loved ones of those extraordinary individuals.[16]

V.
Reliability of Secondary Documentary Evidence

Even when we feel that we can, without apology, make public documents that were originally intended as private or confidential, we must be aware that others may not have felt equally willing to have all private and intimate information made public. I noted above that several Victorian authors destroyed or winnowed their private correspondence to make sure that secrets—some as innocent as Countess Teresa Guiccioli's date of birth and exact age—did not become public. Wordsworth's heirs are on record as having destroyed manuscript letters by William and Dorothy, and they probably also disposed of letters from Annette Vallon; other materials, including one of Dorothy Wordsworth's journals, have been lost since they were first (perhaps selectively) edited in the nineteenth century.[17] Clearly, when we attempt to ascertain the truth about events, relationships, and feelings of the past, we always face the possibility that besides the natural loss of evidence through ignorance and carelessness, knowledgeable individuals — sometimes the authors themselves — may have destroyed or altered significant portions of the record. Here I wish to explore some problems involving evidence based on *private* manuscripts to suggest how careful scholars must be in their reliance on secondary sources. Can we assume that we have reached the truth about a relationship or an event when we rely on the printed texts of letters, or on contemporary manuscript copies, or even on facsimiles of the original documents?

One of the most common defenses of privacy employed by owners of personal letters is to edit, excerpt, or modify the texts of those documents, omitting references that they for some reason do not wish to make public. But for scholars to rely on details of such edited versions without knowing the contents of the originals is often to lean upon a straw. A very clear-cut case involves Shelley's letters to Thomas Jefferson Hogg, his friend from University College, Oxford. Hogg kept Shelley's letters, as well as the drafts of many of his replies, and he published many of Shelley's early letters to him in the two volumes he completed of his aborted *Life of Percy Bysshe Shelley* (1858). In order to protect the living — mainly himself — Hogg edited Shelley's letters a bit, leaving most of the words but reversing many pronouns, so that many of Hogg's own foolish youthful opinions were represented as being Shelley's.

Thirty-four of the forty-four letters from Shelley to Hogg in the years 1810 and 1811 were published directly from the manuscripts and collated with Hogg's published texts in volume 2 of *Shelley and his Circle*. These corrected texts completely undercut most inferences about Shelley's personality and ideas that had been drawn from the published texts—including some elaborate psychosexual analysis—simply because so often Hogg's text demeans Shelley by representing the young Hogg's sentiments as Shelley's while putting Shelley's words and even, on occasion, those of Shelley's sister Elizabeth in his own voice. In a letter of 26 April 26 1811, for example, Shelley tried to calm Hogg down and moderate his friend's infatuation for Elizabeth Shelley (whom he had never met), beginning his letter thus:

> My dear Friend
>   You indulge despair; *why* do you so . . I will not philosophize, it is perhaps a poor way of administering comfort to say that you *ought* not be in need of it . . . wherefore then do I ask *why* you indulge despair.—

In printing the letter in *The Life of Percy Bysshe Shelley*, Hogg changed this passage to the following (italics added to indicate his changes):

> My dear Friend
>   *I* indulge despair. Why do *I* so? I will not philosophise; it is, perhaps, a poor way of administering comfort *to myself* to say, that *I* ought not be in need of it. . . . Wherefore, then, do *you* ask, Why *I* indulge despair?

Such publication was worse than evasive: it was downright subversive. As Cameron points out, "Hogg's picture of himself in his *The Life of Percy Bysshe Shelley* as the rational, sophisticated young man of the world trying to direct the eccentric footsteps of his poet friend has generally been taken at its face value. . . . The manuscripts of these letters, however, show Hogg as a young man of violent and unstable passions who was much more dependent on Shelley than Shelley was on him."[18] I shall add that several would-be biographers and psychological writers on Shelley who depended on the evidence of Hogg's corrupted texts of these letters believed that Shelley had strong but unacknowledged homosexual feelings for Hogg, whereas the aggregate of the corrected texts join other evidence in suggesting that those feelings ran much more strongly in the other direction.

Mary W. Shelley's editing of Shelley's letters provides examples of responsible excisions. Mary Shelley prepared two separate edited texts of Shelley's letters to her. One version, probably done in the 1820s, soon after his death, survives in a number of edited transcripts in her hand; other versions of many of these same letters, with different passages omitted, were published in 1840 in Mary Shelley's edition of Shelley's *Essays, Letters from Abroad, Translations, and Fragments.* In both these edited versions, passages are omitted that allude to private matters that might adversely affect living friends of the Shelleys or harm Mary Shelley's relations with them. (For example, all references that would suggest that Claire Clairmont had borne Byron a child or that Byron had rejected and abused Claire were deleted.) In the later edited versions, the specific omissions changed with the changed circumstances of those individuals mentioned in Shelley's letters.[19] But both edited versions omit material crucial to full biographies of the Shelleys, and until recently neither the transcripts in Mary Shelley's hand nor the later published versions could be used safely without consulting the original manuscripts. The same thing is true of the first published version of Shelley's letters to Leigh Hunt, published by Thornton Hunt and carefully edited to remove, in the wake of Dickens's spiteful portrait of Leigh Hunt as Harold Skimpole in *Bleak House,* all the references to the money that Shelley had given to Hunt. These deletions—most of which were marked by asterisks—were merely tasteful protections of the reputation of a good man temporarily under siege.[20] Leigh Hunt, both during Shelley's lifetime and afterwards, publicly acknowledged his indebtedness to Shelley's generosity, and Hunt's heirs kept intact all the Shelley letters that came into their possession so that later scholars could make public the full record. Indeed, even Thomas Jefferson Hogg kept the manuscripts that showed his dereliction, thereby assuring himself a lasting if clouded place in the annals of Shelley studies. A far more severe problem may exist in the biographies of Stephen Crane, where Thomas Beer, one of Crane's early biographers, published many early letters for which nobody else has seen any original manuscript versions and which the recent editors of Crane's *Correspondence* believe were, in part at least, fabrications by Beer himself.[21]

These and other examples that might be mentioned, including the *public* versions of Shelley's travel letters describing his voyage with Byron around Lake Geneva and the visit to the Vale of Chamouni and Mount Blanc that appeared in the Shelleys' *History of a Six Weeks' Tour* (1817), show that published versions of personal letters, whatever role they may play in the *public* text of the works in which they appear, are not to be confused with, or substituted for, the text in the original manuscript.[22] All editors of *private* documents axiomatically have very sound reasons, some of which I have adduced, for employing tact and discretion in the publication of such documents, and they may well have intervened to muffle or distort the earlier *public* versions of these texts. Editors, biographical scholars, or critics who assume that an available published text represents all there is to know about such a document often find themselves led far away from the truth.

But what about graphic facsimiles? Can they be trusted to yield the essentials of the texts and arrangements of letters and other personal documents? Unfortunately, no, though all of us must depend upon them more often than we would like to. Since all students of manuscripts undoubtedly have a repertoire of anecdotes about mistakes and confusions that have resulted from depending upon photocopies, I shall cite just three examples, each illustrating a different hazard, but by no means exhausting the possibilities for such errors. The travel diary of Maria Gisborne mentioned above was edited for publication by Frederick L. Jones, who had earlier acknowledged his reliance on a microfilm of an unscholarly printed text for his edition of *Mary Shelley's Journal*. In *Maria Gisborne & Edward E. Williams, Shelley's Friends: Their Journals and Letters,* Jones does not specify his authority. But George H.

Ford, who was at the British Museum working on the Gisbornes' journals when Jones's edition appeared, reviewed it for *Modern Philology* in terms that leave no doubt about its inadequacies.[23] Most of Ford's important corrections have never been incorporated into Shelley scholarship, but here I shall note a couple of Ford's general comments on the text:

> It seems likely that Mr. Jones has relied not upon manuscripts but upon microfilm or some other form of copy. He notes, for example, that an extra sheet has been "pasted in the MS book," and he makes a valiant effort to invent a reading for the parts obscured by this sheet (pp. 26–27). In reality, the sheet was pinned into the book, not pasted, and it is easy enough to transcribe what is underneath it. Failure to consult the manuscript may also explain why John Gisborne's journal is described as overflowing "into another notebook" (p. vii), whereas it actually overflowed into forty-one books. (P. 69)

Scholars who rely on photocopies are not only liable to commit more errors of their own but also subject to the errors of photographers and those who arrange and mark the photocopies that are sent to them. In the recent magnificent edition of *Byron's Letters and Journals*—edited largely from photocopies, though, because of Leslie A. Marchand's long and firsthand familiarity with most of the materials, mostly without adverse incident—a failure to check some photocopies sent to the editor that the Pforzheimer Library may have inadequately labeled resulted in textual problems sufficient to warn Romanticists once again not to give absolute credence to secondary sources, even such a fine standard edition as this one. In two instances in volume 7, Marchand has published as separate letters sheets of corrections for *Marino Faliero* that Byron sent to John Murray in the fall of 1820, while publishing as separate from them, under different dates, the gossipy notes to John Murray that occupy the opposite sides of the same two sheets, apparently because the photocopies of the rectos and versos of these two leaves had become separated.[24]

Finally, I turn to an instance, also involving Byron, that

goes beyond the normal hazards of using facsimiles. Perhaps the best-known facsimile of the whole Romantic period is the lithographic reproduction of Byron's letter of 27 April 1819 to the Galignani publishing house in Paris that was used as the frontispiece to the Galignanis' 1826 edition of *The Works of Lord Byron*. This facsimile is of such high quality that dozens of scholars and collectors, as well as and several book dealers, have mistaken it for an original letter and taken it to auction houses, announced the discovery in local newspapers, or otherwise stirred up excitement that turned to chagrin and embarrassment when the truth was revealed. In the absence of the original manuscript, which was not known to be extant, Marchand, like earlier editors of Byron's letters, relied on this extraordinary facsimile for his text. When the Galignanis sold some of their manuscripts at a Paris auction, the original manuscript of this letter was purchased by a private collector, who put it on deposit for a time at the Pierpont Morgan Library. Marchand, more in the attitude of a pilgrim seeking out a relic than of a scholar expecting to find new information, visited the Morgan and compared the original with its famous facsimile. There he found that though the early facsimile *seemed* to reproduce all sections of the letter, including some words that Byron had canceled on the second page, it actually omitted a sentence that began at the bottom of the first page and continued at the top of page 2, while a phrase from the top of the second page was reproduced at the bottom of page 1 to fill out the last line there.[25]

The purpose of Byron's letter was to deny authorship of both *The Vampire* and "an account of my 'residence in the Island of Mitylene.' " At the bottom of the first page and the top of the second, the text of the facsimile—and therefore the text in *Byron's Letters and Journals*—reads: "If the book is clever it would be base to deprive the real writer—whoever he may be—of his honours;—and if stupid—I desire the responsibility of nobody's dullness but my own.——You will excuse | the trouble I give. . . ."[26] The actual manuscript reads: "If the book is clever it would be base to deprive the real writer—whoever he may be—of his honours;—and if stupid—I desire the responsibility of nobody's dullness but my own. — I address | you in English since your Journal is written in that language. — You will excuse the trouble I give. . . ."[27]

Just *how* the Galignanis managed to excise one line and parts of two other lines and move another half-line from the top of page 2 to the bottom of page 1 of the lithographic reproduction, I leave to experts on that medium to explain. *Why* they wanted to do so seems to me easier to understand, if we keep in mind the distinction between *private, confidential,* and *public* correspondence.

Byron's letter is not of a *private* nature, since he is denying authorship of works that had been publicly advertised by the Galignanis as being his, and he obviously does not intend them to keep this fact a secret. That is why the Galignanis felt comfortable in reprinting this letter in facsimile. But the one sentence they excised is of another character. On the one hand, in explaining why he wrote to the Galignani brothers in English, Byron (who was apparently unaware of their English background) suggests that he should have addressed them in French (a language in which he felt himself to be inadequate).[28] Naturally enough, the English Galignanis did not wish to transmit this false impression to their English readers and correspondents. At the same time, those who knew that the Galignani brothers spoke English fluently would see at once from Byron's reference that he was not personally knowledgeable about these booksellers and publishers. And since the booksellers' main purpose in reproducing Byron's letter to them as a frontispiece to their edition of his poetry was to imply that they had a special, close relationship with Lord Byron, they wished to delete the single *personal* detail in his letter that would show the world otherwise. They therefore cleverly excised the one *personal* sentence from the facsimile of the otherwise *public* letter in order to spare, not Byron's feelings, but their own. In so doing, they dashed forever the scholar's confidence in even what seems to be the very best of secondary witnesses, and they illustrated how subtle are the interactions of different functional levels of any document that may be affected not only by the author's intention but also by the response of the intended readers.

MODERN MANUSCRIPTS AND

THE PUBLISHED TEXT

❖

Having examined the differences between private, confidential, and public manuscripts and the need for editors, historical scholars, biographers, and critics to take these distinctions into account when using documentary evidence, let us now consider the relationship of *public* modern manuscripts to published texts. Can understanding the intentional and functional distinctions between documents help us resolve a basic contention among editors of poetry, fiction, and other forms of artistic composition? Which witnesses—manuscripts or printed texts—are intrinsically more likely to have authority as copy-texts?

In the early days of printing and printed books, the printers tried to make books resemble manuscript codexes, designing type to mimic the scribal Gothic, secretary, and italic hands used by producers of the calligraphic books and arranging the columns and pages of type according to the pattern of the scribal texts. In the same manner, those who comprehend the resources and possibilities available in the new electronic technologies tell us that we are not taking full advantage of the natural attributes of the new medium but are designing software that replicates both the benefits and many of the limitations of the age of print. There are similar cultural lags in bibliography, editing, and literary studies that result from the inborn tendency of the human psyche to cling to the com-

INVOICE
can not
be found

fortably familiar. In the early days of bibliography, scholars applied many of the lessons of their study of classical and medieval codexes to their analysis of printed books, only gradually working to analyze the peculiar problems inherent in the various means of mass production—from setting by forms and stop-press corrections in hand-set Renaissance books to the vagaries of correcting texts set by the monotype and linotype machines in the nineteenth and twentieth centuries. In the same way, those who were trained first in the study of classical, medieval, and early Renaissance manuscripts periods or whose studies have centered on the analysis of printed books are liable to bring false analogies to their work with texts based on modern manuscripts.

An indication of this problem is suggested by the title of Jean-Louis Lebrave's interesting essay "Rough Drafts: A Challenge to Uniformity in Editing," which treats the difficulty of presenting rough drafts *(brouillons, Arbeitsmanuskripte)* in such a way as both to suggest their own temporal order and to relate their texts to those of the later, revised versions of the same works.[1] Lebrave declares that the solution involves a computerized "dictionary" in which all cancellations, substitutions, and insertions in the text are keyed in the order in which they occurred in the document so that different combinations of these variants can be called up to recreate various stages of the text as it evolved. He thus ultimately answers his own title by arguing that the computerized study of drafts seeks, not "uniformity," but multeity. Late in his paper, Lebrave remarks that "for most purposes, one needs not only an edition, but also a facsimile, and even facsimiles happen to be far from an exact reproduction of the original" (p. 141).

The attempt to present a variety of manuscripts in photofacsimile editions in ways that display the anomalies of their originals has for several years occupied me and twenty-five other scholar-critics who have worked on one or more volumes of *The Bodleian Shelley Manuscripts* and *The Manuscripts of the Younger Romantics.*[2] To foster fidelity to the wide range of manuscripts that appear in the series—from the large, loose bifolia that Byron employed to transcribe his later poems and dramas to the small pocket notebooks in which Shelley drafted his—Garland Publishing and I have encouraged editors to suggest innovations in the presentation of different manuscripts and their accompanying transcriptions and textual notes. One notebook in the Huntington Library, Shelley first used from one end before turning it upside down and using it from the other end, making the "back" of the blank notebook as viewed from one end another "front" when read from the other. In editing it, Mary A. Quinn arranged the photofacsimiles and her transcriptions of the first half "rightside up" with regard to title page and front matter, and the latter half, on which Shelley's text was *reverso* (i.e., "upside down" and sequenced in the other direction), she placed in exactly that position and order. To facilitate use of the textual and informational notes to each part of the manuscript notebook in conjunction with the pages to which they refer, she grouped the pages of notes in the middle of the bound volume, with those referring to the first, "rightside up" half of the manuscript running in the same direction and those commenting on the *reverso* section upside down and progressing in the opposite direction.[3] Just as the diversity of modern manuscripts (compared with the vast majority of scribal manuscripts from earlier eras) forces editors to rethink the possible shapes of the media in which we reproduce them, so we must also rethink the nature of these manuscripts, freed from the dogmas derived from analogies with earlier manuscripts, from the study of books, or even from the use of the electronic technologies that are beginning to influence our patterns of thinking.

I.
Polished Private and Confidential Manuscripts

Does a modern fair-copy manuscript, when prepared by an author or his authorized amanuensis and corrected or approved by the author as copy for the printer, have the same kind of authority that an authorized final manual transcription of a poem intended as a public copy had during the medieval or Renaissance period? Does it have the same authority as, say, a text now prepared by an author on a word processor and transmitted to a publisher on a diskette as the basis for a computer-set book? It is demonstrable, I believe, that after the age of printing had been fully established and authors realized that their final manuscripts were way stations on the road to a perfected text, rather than the thing itself, the manuscript no longer carried the same textual authority that it once had, even when it represented the author's final involvement in such matters as the orthography and punctuation of most of the text. If I am correct, then the program fostered by Fredson Bowers and his followers to try to move behind first editions to recover the nature of the authors' holograph press copies has in many instances been a mistaken effort.[4] To say that when modern authors send their work to press, they expect it to be changed from the form of the manuscripts in which they first submit it, anticipating—and in many cases hoping—that changes in the text or its presentation will be introduced by the printers or the publishers, does not mean that *all* manuscripts of the nineteenth century lack the final authority that we now accord to printed works. But, paradoxically, the manuscripts most likely to deserve the appellation "final authority" are often documents prepared by the author *without* an immediate intention of publishing, in many cases, poems or other compositions that were intended for the perusal of a few specific individuals—in short, *private* or *confidential* documents.

Let us begin (appropriately) with *Volume the First,* one of Jane Austen's early manuscript miscellanies now in the Bodleian Library. Originally edited for publication by R. W. Chapman, this copybook, measuring approximately 8 × 6¼ inches, contains—as Chapman and later scholars agree—fair copies of some of Austen's earliest writings that were not meant for publication. In view of some remarks in the preceding chapter, the conclusion of Chapman's preface to his edition of this manuscript deserves quotation as an index to the state of discussions of questions of confidentiality in 1925:

It will always be disputed whether such effusions as these ought to be published; and it may be that we have enough already of Jane Austen's early scraps. The author of the MEMOIR [Austen's nephew James Edward Austen-Leigh] thought a very brief specimen sufficient. But perhaps the question is hardly worth discussion. For if such manuscripts find their way into great libraries, their publication can hardly be prevented. The only sure way to prevent it is the way of destruction, which no one dare take.[5]

Since Chapman presents the printed text of *Volume the First* very literally, it is possible to tell even from it that Jane Austen's manuscript is a thoroughly finished and polished one, at least as polished (given her age and experience of books at the time) as that of *Lady Susan,* which Austen wrote out fair after 1805, perhaps with an eye to its publication, and as polished as most press-copy manuscripts of the period. Like those other press copies, *Volume the First* includes many ampersands, an occasional misspelling (e.g., "bel*eiv*'d" in the "Song" on p. 7), and numerals that in a printed text would have been spelled out (pp. 7 and 8). When Austen copied out these materials, she had no aspirations to publish any of her writing and certainly not these "trifles" (as her sister Cassandra describes them), which were written for the confidential amusement of Cassandra, their brother Charles, and other family members and friends. Since some neighbors and acquaintances whom she disliked seem to have been targets of her satirical thrusts, the manuscript was clearly not intended to circulate beyond Jane Austen's circle of like-minded intimates, who alone could understand the point of these barbs and share the humor of them. In short, the manuscript is a *confidential* one. The care that Austen exerted in its presentation, with its accurate quotation marks and clear section divisions—like the neatness of late medieval or early Renaissance English commonplace books and family poetic miscellanies—derives from the fact that the writer never expected the manuscript to be superseded by a more authoritative printed text. Such a manuscript had to be more carefully prepared than a press copy, because it would neither be vetted by publisher's readers and compositors nor corrected in proof.

Similarly, among the neatest and most nearly perfect holograph manuscripts of Shelley's poetry are his fair copies of the yearning and very *private* lyrics that he addressed to Jane Williams in 1822. These holographs—known as the "Trelawny manuscripts" because they ended up in the possession of Edward John Trelawny, rather than the Shelley heirs—were eventually donated to major libraries in England and Scotland as prime examples of Shelley's autograph.[6] They are in every respect as clear, neat, and accurate as any of Shelley's holograph press copies. And the reason is not hard to find: while he was in Italy, Shelley (like Wordsworth and Byron) preferred to have Mary Shelley prepare the press copies of his *public* poems. He transcribed the final texts only of poems that contained very private matter that he thought might irritate his wife, such as the press copy for *Julian and Maddalo* and "Athanase: A Fragment" and lyrics addressed and sent to other women, such as Sophia Stacey, Teresa ("Emilia") Viviani, and Jane Williams.[7] (There are, of course, a few exceptions, including some short poems that Shelley sent to Hunt for publication in the *Indicator,* including holographs of two poems recently acquired by the Pforzheimer Collection.) Shelley did not give his lyrics inspired by Jane Williams to Mary Shelley or anyone else to copy, nor did he intend to send them to press. He therefore prepared his fair copies more carefully than the manuscripts that he sent to press, which—whether or not he would have an opportunity to read proofs—would be looked over by someone else who could catch and correct slips of the pen.

A contrasting example is provided by Byron's press copies of *Beppo* and *Marino Faliero* (both in the Pforzheimer Collection), in which he left certain problems unresolved until he read the proofs. In a number of instances, for example, Byron could not decide on the exact diction and left alternative words or phrases in his manuscripts, from which John Murray and his advisers were to make an initial choice for the press; then Byron had a chance to look at the poem as a whole again in its typeset form and either to ratify or modify the readings as they pleased him. Although Byron prepared his own press copies on extra large sheets of paper, in *Beppo* and *Marino Faliero* he still relied on the ambiguity of his handwriting to save himself from having to make some hard decisions about the punctuation. His periods and commas are often indistinguishable, and by leaving them so, he again shifted the burden for making the first choice to the compositor at Thomas Davison's print shop or to John Murray and his colleagues.[8] Because Byron was a best-selling author, his publisher would send him proofs as often as he wished and permit him both to alter these at will and to supplement or alter the text after its first publication, for correction in later editions (for Murray had learned from the experience of publishing *The Giaour* and other early works that substantial revisions in later editions merely increased the sales of Byron's poems).

But while Byron, backed by his commercial success, could thus be relatively casual in preparing his manuscripts for the press, neither Shelley nor Charles Ollier, Shelley's small, undercapitalized publisher, could afford the expense of mailing proofs between England and Italy. Shelley therefore learned that in order to approach his personal standards of accuracy (which were higher than Byron's), he must either supervise the printing himself in Italy (as he did with both *The Cenci* and *Adonais*) or else prepare his press copy so accurately that it could be followed without alteration. Even then, to reduce the cost of postage for himself and Ollier, Shelley had his writings copied for the press on small slips of paper torn from larger sheets. Mary Shelley or Claire Clairmont usually wrote out most of those final copies to mail to Ollier, because their handwriting was more legible than Shelley's when reduced in size to fit the lines of poetry onto the small slips of paper.[9] Because they are so tiny and crowded, these press copies surely caused problems for compositors—as some have also caused problems for more recent editors. If only from the point of view of their relative spaciousness and clarity, then, the holograph poems that Shelley gave to such friends as Edward and Jane Williams are among the least ambiguous and most nearly perfected of all his manuscripts. They are so partly *because* they were *private* documents that Shelley himself prepared, knowing that there would be no wife, friend, publisher, or compositor to look over the text and catch his errors.

I take my third example of a carefully executed *private* or *confidential* modern manuscript from a lesser work in the Pforzheimer Collection. Sometime in the 1830s or 1840s, William Makepeace Thackeray invited Leigh Hunt to dine with him on New Year's Day, urbanely phrasing his note to disguise its rhymes, so that it would appear to be a routine formal invitation, rather than a clever short poem:

> My dear Hunt
> Though we never meet, we should. If you
> would and if you could will you take your dinner
> here on the first day of the year? And believe me
> Hunt my dear Yours forever and a day,
>   Doubleyouem Thackeray.[10]

This clever note (which, since a former owner had framed it, was for years displayed on the wall at the old Pforzheimer Library premises at 41 East 42nd Street) is obviously a *private* manuscript. Yet it was prepared as carefully as what, in fact, it also is: a small work of art, somewhat less ephemeral than a cleverly decorated birthday cake. Presumably, Thackeray was not looking for immortality with these functional verses, though he was certainly trying to demonstrate his wit and talent to Leigh Hunt, who by the late 1830s was considered by the rising literary generation a martyr-hero of the free press and a grand old man of letters.[11] For this reason, as in the drawings that Thackeray added to his personal letters, he executed this personal poetic note with greater care, perhaps, than he might devote to some sections of his manuscripts for the press.[12] Thus, once again, we see that *public* manuscripts are distinguished from other manuscripts neither by artistry nor by care of preparation but only by the scope and nature of the intended audience. If we knew that Thackeray expected Hunt to be pleased with the invitation and to show it to other friends as a sample of Thackeray's wit (and fondness for Hunt), he could be said to have conceived of it as a *confidential* rather than a strictly *private* manuscript. But publication of the invitation any time soon after its composition would have been seen as a tasteless irrelevancy (as were Leigh Hunt's essentially private poems about his son John that he published in the *Examiner*). Only at the proper distance of time, when a broad spectrum of the reading public begins to take a direct interest in personalia relating to author and recipient, can such ephemera pass for *public* documents.

II.
Transformations of Private Texts into Public Ones

In the publication of personal documents, as in some other private concerns, timing is everything. Personal revelations that are proper in one setting may be gauche in another. Though my earlier remarks about the publication of Joyce's most intimate love letters in the most widely circulated selection of his letters and about the public use of Richard Ellmann's private and confidential correspondence so soon after *his* death to bolster one side in a public quarrel about the private or confidential motives of living scholars and publishers may seem antiquated in the light of such more recent examples as the publication of John Cheever's private diaries and the contents of the audiotapes Anne Sexton recorded for her personal psychotherapist,[13] I meant to suggest that tact in the publication, rather than destruction or suppression, was the proper answer to the question how to deal with private and confidential documents. Personal privacy and scholarly tact remain matters of situational ethics, and perhaps all that one can say categorically about the issue is this: Any private or confidential document can honorably be made public if the document is published at the right time, for the appropriate audience, and introduced by the editor with the proper tact. As I suggested, Ellmann showed the proper attitude toward Joyce's letters, and he did not publish them too hastily. Prevented by the Joyce estate from publishing these letters earlier, as part of the larger scholarly collection, Ellmann may have felt that he was forced to include them in the popular selection of the letters. But it still may seem a lapse of taste for the publisher—perhaps with Ellmann's acquiescence—to have advertised these letters on the dust jacket in order to stimulate sales of the volume.

Different degrees of tact may be requisite in different historical periods. In the case of Jane Austen's juvenilia, her nephew did not publish them in full when his memoir appeared in 1870, possibly because at that date the novelist's reputation was not sufficiently secure to assure her earliest work a fair hearing and because her nephew feared that his publication of these works might be seen as an act of special pleading by the author's family. But when R. W. Chapman published *Volume the First* in 1925, not only were Austen's novels being acknowledged as classics but (as Chapman's preface implies) the acquisition of the notebook by the Bodleian both preserved the manuscript for posterity and conferred on it a new status as an artifact of lasting intrinsic value.

Mary Shelley's editing of Shelley's works shows similar concern for the feelings of the potential audience and tact toward those feelings in the interest of promoting Shelley's long-term reputation. She withheld some of Shelley's poems and early prose tracts from her collective editions of 1839 and 1840 because she feared that at that time the bellicose tone of his early prose, *Queen Mab,* and such later poems as *Peter Bell the Third* and *Swellfoot the Tyrant* might hurt Shelley's reputation rather than help the public to accept him as a great poet. As soon as Mary Shelley realized that the reviewers and public were willing to accept this work, she added as much of it as seemed to her worthy of his genius, though she favored his poetry over his early prose.[14] Mary Shelley published Shelley's personal poems to Jane Williams as soon as was appropriate, drawing the texts of some from Shelley's rough-draft notebooks and others from texts first published in various journals by other friends of Shelley's. She even reprinted a lyric called "To the Queen of My Heart," which turned out to have been published as a hoax by a young man who wanted to prove that he could write in Shelley's manner.[15] Mary W. Shelley quite properly disguised the identities of the recipients of Shelley's personal lyrics addressed to other women simply by giving them such titles as "To a Lady. With a Guitar" and "To——." Since she herself was the person who might have been expected to take the most offense at the existence as well as the publication of these poems, she was violating no rights of privacy so long as she suppressed the names of the other women involved.

As time passed, people who might once have lost status because of their friendships with Shelley began to gain from their associations with him, and there came to be less and less reason for omitting their names or disguising the distant past. Shelley himself had usually been discreet in his later years; his early letters to Elizabeth Hitchener, for example, did not surface until near the end of the century, and the letters to Harriet Shelley until the 1930s, by which time all those people who might have been personally embarrassed by the revelations were no longer living. By that time, also, Shelley's poetic reputation was so well established that his youthful errors could be put into the perspective of his whole life, works, and influence. By such commonsense observation of the operations of what Shelley in *Prometheus Unbound* terms "Fate, Time, Occasion, Chance, and Change," Mary Shelley and others among the survivors of the Romantic era were able to maintain their honesty and forthrightness about the dead poet without violating basic human obligations either to foreground his larger literary achievement or to protect the welfare and reputations of the living.

Between 1855 and 1860, however, when Thomas Love Peacock first published his *Memoirs of Percy Bysshe Shelley* as a series of articles in *Fraser's Magazine,* some thirty years had passed since Shelley's death. Although Peacock—by then a senior member of the establishment at the East India Company—had not basically compromised his early values (some of which differed from Shelley's, in any case), he knew about Thomas Jefferson Hogg's alteration of Shelley's letters, and as Nicholas A. Joukovsky has recently suggested, at least one passage in Hogg's *Life of Percy Bysshe Shelley* was about some of Peacock's early financial problems, though his identity was masked. Peacock and his mother had suffered from such dire poverty in his years of early manhood that, as Joukovsky has revealed, he may have been on the verge of committing suicide before Shelley came to his aid with a regular stipend, as Hogg hints.[16] Later, Peacock's wife suffered from mental illness. Thus Peacock, more than most members of Shelley's circle, appreciated the need for reserve and discretion about private matters. He underscores the universality of his theme of privacy by opening his *Memoirs of Percy Bysshe Shelley* with an epigraph from Rousseau, a writer whose *Confessions* had made him a byword for indiscretion. To a woman who sent Rousseau a copy of a brochure about his private life that she had published after he had entertained her, he wrote a note that may be translated thus: "Rousseau, who does not receive any authors, thanks Madame——for her kindness, and begs her not to come to his home again." Peacock then develops the theme of privacy and discretion through the first seven paragraphs of the *Memoirs,* including this passage from paragraph three:

> This appetite for gossip about notorieties being once created in the "reading public," there will be always found persons to minister to it; and among the volunteers of this service, those who are best informed and who most valued the departed will probably not be the foremost. Then come biographies abounding with errors; and then, as a matter of defence perhaps, comes on the part of friends a tardy and more authentic narrative. This is at best, as Mr. Hogg describes it, a "difficult and delicate task." But it is always a matter of choice and discretion. No man is bound to write the life of another. No man who does so is bound to tell the public all he knows. On the contrary, he is bound to keep to himself whatever may injure the interests or hurt the feelings of the living, especially when the latter have in no way injured or calumniated the dead, and are not necessarily brought be-

fore the tribunal of public opinion in the character of either plaintiffs or defendants.[17]

The passage quoted may well have been partly a comment on Hogg's unethical use of sources. Having seen documents so misused, Peacock chose another alternative to either publishing in full or misrepresenting the documentary evidence: he destroyed it. Peacock sometime before 1838 carried out an exchange with Mary Shelley in which she seems to have given him a large number of his own letters to Shelley in return for a comparable quantity of Shelley's letters to him; after this exchange, Peacock owned all letters by Shelley or himself that mentioned Shelley's financial assistance to Peacock before he began his tenure at East India House. These he seems to have destroyed. Like the other Victorians whom I mentioned above (see chapter 2), Peacock must have felt that such pruning of the archives was the only way to be sure of keeping his family's private traumas from public view. Thus, as I have suggested, the indiscreet—in Hogg's case, the unscrupulous—use of private letters and documents by those writing biographies of the Romantics led to the destruction of important information about many of those who lived to see such misuse. As I shall now suggest, the attempts of modern textual scholars to substitute for an author's own preferred *public* texts of his poems versions drawn from his earlier *private* or *confidential* manuscripts could lead some modern authors to destroy the valuable information contained in these even more important materials.

III.

Recognizing the Author's Authority

Many literary documents—and, I dare say, several historical ones—exist in two or more *public* versions. The poems of Pope, Wordsworth, Coleridge, Byron, Tennyson, Yeats, and Auden and the novels of Scott, Manzoni, Balzac, and Henry James all provide instances where an early published text was supplemented, revised, or even totally rewritten by the author in a different dialect or idiom for republication later in life. Sometimes, as with Scott's Magnum Opus edition, one motive was gain, the author and publisher desiring to sell copies of the new edition to those who already owned copies of the earlier text.[18] But in a great many cases the writers had either changed their minds about the issues that had engendered the writings or, with the advantage of hindsight, believed that they could express the same ideas better through a different presentation. Still, since the two (or more) versions of their poems or novels were prepared as *public* entities and offered by them to readers for their response and judgment, there was no gainsaying the prerogative of readers to decide which versions of the works *they* preferred. Once authors release their work to the public at large, they can no longer exercise primary control over its course of life.

In some cases, authors may release writings to publishers with certain expectations of what the public will see, but through censorship, editorial interference, or incompetence in the means of production, the works are so deflected away from the authors' prior intentions that they disown the published versions. Such was the case with Tolstoy's *What Is Art?* Tolstoy is reported to have declared the English translation by Aylmer Maude (1898), which incorporated the author's last revisions, to be the only approved version, in preference to the censored Russian edition.[19] In this case, Tolstoy's late additions and declared preference prevent a scholar from returning to the Russian published edition for a totally authoritative text.

On the other hand, have critics or editors the right to discard a great writer's final text, arrived at after years of contemplation, consultation with other noted writers, and at least three thorough revisions of the entire work? Instead of fulfilling the unambiguous wishes of the author, who revised his text and prepared his final manuscript for posthumous publication, completing that preparation a full eleven years before his death, some critics and editors declare that *they* know better than William Wordsworth which was the best version of *The Prelude* to present to the public. Some substitute for it the transcript of an intermediate draft version prepared in 1805–6, even though Wordsworth continued to restructure and revise it as late as the 1830s. Editors of anthologies have even replaced Wordsworth's twelve-book text with an un-formed, two-part ur-draft dating from 1798–99 that the poet used as raw material for some passages in the poem as it developed over the next four decades. What might William Wordsworth have done with these earlier manuscripts had he known that a series of not-so-harmless drudges in the academy would set themselves up as the arbiters concerning which parts of his finished poems would be available to the public and which would be cast aside in favor of discarded and rejected versions? How much would we scholars have lost in our com-prehension of his artistry and life had he felt compelled to destroy the record of the childhood of his greatest poem, lest later readers take it upon themselves to use that record to denigrate the man it became? And how much harm might such feckless editing bring to the study of twentieth-century poetry and prose if the writers of our day, many of them students of these arrogant editors, destroy their early versions when they realize that some academics cannot keep their pedagogic hands off the works of the world's creative spirits and—if they cannot stifle the originality of such writers in their classrooms—will later try to replace it with their own limited taste through editorial decisions when the authors are dead and can no longer defend their offspring?

As we have seen, the growing monetary value of manuscript archives may slow or inhibit the destruction of early drafts and rejected versions. Such materials may be kept as an in-surance policy for the spouses and children of some distin-guished writers, and a great many undistinguished ones will beg institutions to accept their papers in the hope that posterity will take some interest in them. But some of the best artists among living writers—those who care more for the integrity of their writing than for the price of their table scraps, or those who are so financially secure that they have no need to sell their souls to the academy—may well decide to destroy anything that a so-called textual scholar may "discover" to set up in the place of the poems that the artist wrote and approved.

I was once told that the Huntington Library's collection of the literary manuscripts of Wallace Stevens is very much in this vein, consisting largely of typescripts of final versions of his poems. James Thorpe assures me that this is not true, that it contains early notebooks and other interesting materials, though he could not swear that Holly Stevens had not pruned some parts of the collection. But even if the first story, which I heard from a Stevens scholar, were mistaken, we can imagine that some artists now living who may share Stevens's desire for privacy and who enjoy comparable financial security might well consider ridding their archives of materials that are either too revelatory or more likely to enhance the career of an academic researcher than to add to their own poetic stature.

The saddest thing about this situation is that if scholars and critics were content to fulfill their proper roles, without trying to usurp that of the creative artists, there need be no conflict between them. If scholars simply presented private materials tactfully and published the drafts and rejected versions of the writings, not as rivals of the authorial texts but for their value in revealing the growth and development of the authors and the workings of the creative process, and if critics could learn to comment on these implications without pretending that their taste is superior to that of the writers, there would be credit and livelihoods for scholars and critics, illumination for readers, and enhanced interest and renewed acclaim for the authors. It seems unlikely, in the course of human nature, that academic editors will gain in modesty and admit that their literary tastes are an ill substitute for those of the artists. But by instructing editors and critics of the future to observe the simple distinction between *private, confidential,* and *public* literary manuscripts, we may yet succeed in forestalling the misguided attempts of scholars to use the writers' preliminary worksheets and unauthorized discards as the basis for questioning the fundamental aesthetic intelligence of the finest writers of each age.

IV.
The Site of Authority in Public Works

Because critics and explicators who expound works for other readers bring to their readings a variety of private experiences into which they translate the works, no single interpretation of a truly masterful poem or fiction will satisfy most other readers, although each reading may teach them to see new things that they accept as valid. This great diversity of response makes it impossible to construct a theory of interpretation or valorization of literature based solely or even primarily on reader response to a work. Not even a consensus of the self-appointed "interpretive community" of experts can establish the meaning of a work, because usually such a consensus represents a dead orthodoxy that drains the work of art of all vitality and embalms it in a museum atmosphere. For example, at the end of the eighteenth century, the established "interpretive community"—including William Cowper and William Hayley, Milton's current biographers and editors—were proclaiming that John Milton and his poetry were fully in tune with traditional English and Christian values as established by the Glorious Revolution of 1688 and were opposed to the godless Jacobinism of revolutionary France. But at the same time, Blake, Wordsworth, Coleridge, and Southey were rediscovering Milton as a revolutionary regicide; a few years later, after Wordsworth, Coleridge, and Southey had gone on to accept the vision of Milton as English patriot vis-à-vis imperialistic France, Byron, Shelley, and Keats extended and deepened the exploration, begun by the elder Romantics, of the more subversive implications of Milton's thought and art.

But if the diverse responses of differing readers cannot establish a single, agreed-upon meaning of a work (unless we relativistically agree to recognize the existence of dozens or hundreds of works of art in a single text), what about two other possible loci for the meaning of the work of art? Does such meaning lie in the mind of the author or in the linguistic structure of the text itself? Neither in itself can be easily established, as may be seen in the complexities of eclectic editing under the Greg-Bowers-Tanselle theory of textual scholarship, the aim of which is to establish an ideal "work" out of a series of botched artifacts (imperfect "texts") through recovering the heretofore lost intentions of the author.[20] In fact, eclectic editing might be seen as an informed variety of reader-response theory, since the emendations that the editor supplies to "correct" the readings surviving in individual texts of the work are bound to differ from editor to editor, such corrections depending in part upon subjective interpretations of the posited "work."

Hershel Parker, a theorist who in some ways carries to its ultimate conclusion Bowers's arguments in favor of using the author's manuscript over printed text, argues that while the editor should begin with the earliest complete text of the work, the version produced during the height of the author's most involved and inspired creativity, it is a mistake to pay attention to most later revisions of the work, because the author's later thoughts, when he or she is not creatively engaged, usually fail to match the virtues of the original conception.[21] (Parker once informed Norman Mailer that he had ruined one of his own novels through later revision.) Yet in spite of aberrations in theory and practice among the theorists and editors of the New Bibliography, we know that Tanselle, Parker and their predecessors are right in pointing to the manifest imperfections that mar most, if not all, documents that attempt to embody the ideal "work." In short, there is no easily ascertainable single authority: the writer is now dead after trying to express himself or herself in a series of publications (and, perhaps, a series of comments on them); the texts of the work are, perhaps, multiple and more or less imperfect, some of them produced by the fertile imaginations of the textual critics and editors who were supposed to recover them from the errors of the past; and readers, informed and uninformed, produce an ever-changing cacophony of interpretations.

My philosophy of literature has always been a relational one, trying to keep in focus, first, the writer's apparent intentions insofar as these can be determined both from historical, cultural, and biographical evidence and from the text and the literary codes and traditions that it embodies; second, the textual evidence of the message as it is embodied in specific documents or "texts"; and third, the intended audience and its responses, as well as the relevant responses of other audiences in other times and places.[22] But the best starting point for a search for the "real" text of a *public* work of art would seem to reside either in the author's last holograph manuscript (or an authorially approved press-copy transcription), if the work was not printed during his or her lifetime, or in the printed text nearest to the latest version of the work released to its intended public. Naturally, I would not accept as authoritative any features that an author later specifically rejected as incorrect (as determined, for example, by holograph corrections in copies of the printed work or by explicit references to the limitations of the printed edition). But to allow an editor to "correct" a text by introducing readings for which no documentary evidence exists, based only on the subjective editorial inference of what some lost document may have contained, seems to me dangerous at best and hubristic as carried out by most editors.

Finally, if there survive *both* a manuscript copy prepared (or approved) by an author for the press *and* the printed edition prepared from that manuscript with the consultation of the author, which would probably provide the preferred copy-text document? By failing to recognize the nature of modern manuscripts as unfinished, transitional documents, some editors following the Greg-Bowers orthodoxy have sought to unravel all the work that most authors of the age of print expected editors, typesetters, and proofreaders to contribute to the text. At issue here is not (as Tanselle frequently argues) whether one is interested in studying the preferences of the individual genius or the implications of a socialized text. The nature of a great percentage of press-copy manuscripts during the Enlightenment and Romantic periods of the age of modern manuscripts shows clearly that the author's intention included the expectation, or at least the hope, of correcting proofs personally and thus viewing and perfecting the text after it had been embodied in the printed form in which it would be presented to the world at large. Even beyond the matter of the proofs, authors expected that certain changes and improvements would be made by those whose primary business was to transform the author's manuscript into a published book.

This focus brings us to a group of recent textual theorists who advocate a more socialized view of the creative process and, consequently, of the text and the work. These textual critics—and Jerome J. McGann, D. F. McKenzie, and Jack Stillinger are among them[23]—are less concerned with the mental intentions of "individual authors" (the very existence of whom as separable entities some theorists deny on philosophical grounds). Instead, they see the work as representing the expression of a society, or as an upwelling of the pressures of social conditions and events of the age, or as the product of cooperative efforts by groups of fellow laborers. To a textual theorist of this perspective, a successful literary work does not express the private view of an individual whom we call "the author" but rather embodies the voice of a cultural moment or a communal group. Publication during the era of the "Gutenberg Galaxy" is thus viewed as a social act, with the involvement of a patron, a bookseller, or a publisher, as well as compositors, printers, proofreaders, and other technical expediters of the means of production. When we add to these active participants the social limitations imposed by governmental and religious establishments or at least by the prejudices and expectations of a reading public, we may concede that the work of art that emerges from this process of socialization is not that which began in the private world of the individual author (who was, of course, also formed by impinging social, intellectual, and ideological forces during his or her maturation as a writer and throughout the conception and gestation of the particular work of art).

This view of the literary work as a social product seems to me to add a useful dimension to the identification of the work of art. To create a work intended for the general public more than *implies* a willingness to meet the demands of the system of distribution: it *assumes* such a willingness. But though we may accept the need to include the social dimensions of the process of literary creation and production, we must not fall into the error of thinking that institutions are the creative authors of books. At the lowest level we know that the process of socialization often leads to simple errors rather than to a widening of the social focus. When Swift shrouds his message in irony in the early paragraphs of *A Modest Proposal . . .*, he may be said to be socializing his message by evading the rejection that his protest would have encountered from English authorities with power to rectify the situation had he said directly that English exploitation of the Irish people was outrageously immoral. That kind of socialization becomes embodied as part of the author's intention and would not be affected under either theory of the authoritative text. But when, through a careless mistake in the transmission of the text, the order of two chapters of Henry James's *Ambassadors* was reversed in what became the standard text, or when typographical errors replace words that make more sense in the thematic contexts, such distortions have nothing to do with the legitimate process of socialization but are simply errors and ought to be rooted out, whether they originated in the carelessness of the author in transcribing his text or in the ignorance of compositors who set words that they happened to know, rather than unfamiliar words in the author's manuscript.[24]

Between such clear-cut cases there exist many murky areas where, according to the best available evidence, the personal preference of the author seems to lean in one direction, while the public text that emerged from the process of socialization says something else. In a number of instances the proper solution (as I suggested in "Versioning: The Presentation of Multiple Texts")[25] may be to publish facsimiles and/or diplomatic transcriptions of all interesting versions of a work so that those who wish to study the author's feelings and ideas or the growth and development of the literary work will have available the evidence of authorial intention, while those who wish to trace the impact of the socializing process can compare the author's last version with that which emerged after his friends, printer, and publisher finished with it.

But because many students and general readers will not have the time or interest to compare several versions, scholars must still prepare critical texts for anthologies and single-text editions of a poet's works that choose between the authority of the writer and that of the social process. In such instances, I would favor basing the texts on versions that the author accepted as his or her public texts once they were circulated rather than on prepublication manuscripts. I make this choice on the basis of the distinction that has been made between *private, confidential,* and *public* manuscripts. To intend that a work be made public is (almost always) to will that it undergo the process of socialization.[26] An author who sends a work to press understands that it will come out looking different from the way it appeared in the manuscript. To follow the fragments of an authorial manuscript as copy-text for part of the text while accepting the more polished text from the first edition where the manuscript does not exist may be likened to sending a child out to meet the public in a clean shirt, necktie, and the jacket of his best suit, while leaving him in his pajama bottoms; and to revise the other parts to conform to the manuscript fragments is like tearing off the dress clothes and sewing a new pajama top. The printed edition was the clothing that the author not only expected for his work but went to publisher and printer, those tailors of texts, to acquire. To ignore this fundamental element of authorial intention, while quibbling about hyphens and other minutiae of orthography and punctuation, seems to be swallowing camels while straining for gnats.

V.

Press-Copy Manuscript versus Printed Text

As with other debatable issues, partisans of one view or another are apt to try to win the battle in advance by renaming the elements in the argument. "Setting copy" has become a common term for what I call "press copy," particularly among those who take the line held by Fredson Bowers and G. Thomas Tanselle that authorially approved manuscripts sent to press usually have precedence over the resulting first editions. What the term "setting copy" implies, of course, is that the author did not intend any editorial changes or corrections of that manuscript to be made from the time the author gave it his or her final approval until the compositor set type from it. But, of course, with the advent of editorial procedures at the publisher's office, including copy editing, the term "setting copy" may be misleading. For after the manuscript initially went to press, most authors expected to see either copy-edited manuscript or a set of proofs. George Crabbe, for example, sent his manuscript of *Tales of the Hall* (1819) to press only to rewrite it extensively through a series of successive printed proofs. (A bound collection, including both Crabbe's original manuscript and successive proofs that contain and are accompanied by numerous holograph additions and deletions, is in the Pforzheimer Collection, New York Public Library.) More recent authors—Thomas Wolfe comes to mind—learned to expect their manuscripts to undergo several stages of revision between the time when they were given to the publisher and the time when the books appeared in print. Thus, just as manuscripts of the eighteenth and nineteenth centuries were sometimes sent to the print shop, as twentieth-century authors sometimes send handwritten copy to professional typists (i.e., to provide readable copies that can then be revised and corrected for publication), the text that many a successful modern author submits to a publisher is a negotiating copy, the purpose of which is to find out whether the projected book is acceptable and how much will be paid for it. Author and editor(s) together then work out the final text.

Many authors who sent a *public* work to press in the era of the Gutenberg Galaxy[27] thus did not consider even their last revised and corrected press-copy manuscripts to embody the form in which they expected or intended it to meet that public. In some previous reviews and polemical essays where I was reacting to the specific practices of other editors of Shelley or other eighteenth- and nineteenth-century writers, I argued on the other side of the question, asserting that editors were obliged to rely on the author's press-copy manuscript for most features of the text. One reward I reaped from considering the subject of modern manuscripts comprehensively while preparing the lectures on which this volume is based was to learn to correct such errors in my earlier work and to reach what now seems to me a more cogent conclusion.

Some authors, including Samuel Johnson, Byron, and Keats, came to expect substantial help from amanuenses, editors, typesetters, and proofreaders, if only to set their first thoughts in type so that they could revise heavily at the proof stage. Dr. Johnson's famous remarks on the punctuation of Shakespeare's plays in his preface to his edition of Shakespeare suggest what his attitude toward the punctuation of his own works must often have been:

> In restoring the author's works to their integrity, I have considered the punctuation as wholly in my power; for what could be their care of colons and commas, who corrupted words and sentences. Whatever could be done by adjusting points is therefore silently performed, in some plays with much diligence, in others with less; it is hard to keep a busy eye steadily fixed upon evanescent atoms, or a discursive mind upon evanescent truth.[28]

Thus, first the various editors of the Yale Johnson and later many of us who held to the doctrine that *modernizing* is *vandalizing* came to realize that the arguments for maintaining the punctuation of the original editions of Johnson's work could not stand on the issue of authorial choice or preference. In many cases, at least, he clearly left this and other details to the discretion of the compositors and the proofreaders in the print shop.[29]

Byron also, as I mentioned earlier, relied on the editorial assistance of John Murray's aids, such as William Gifford, to help him choose between alternative phrasings and to judge expressions about which he could not decide, and he used the printing process to help him correct and normalize his orthography and punctuation. As Jack Stillinger has demonstrated both in his discussions of Keats's texts in *The Texts of Keats's Poems* and, more graphically, in seven volumes of edited facsimiles of the primary manuscript sources for Keats's texts that have appeared in *The Manuscripts of the Younger Romantics*,[30] Keats depended upon a series of friends, including his schoolmaster Charles Cowden Clarke, Leigh Hunt, John Hamilton Reynolds, John Taylor, Richard Woodhouse, and Charles Armitage Brown, for help in correcting his grammar, diction, orthography, and punctuation, as well as for advice on what subjects were proper and acceptable in poetry. The case of *Isabella; or, The Pot of Basil* is typically complicated. Though Keats made a holograph fair copy from his draft, the copy that went to press was developed in the following circuitous fashion: Keats lent his fair-copy holograph to John Hamilton Reynolds, who showed it to Richard Woodhouse, a lawyer who not only greatly admired Keats but also acted as a literary adviser to the firm of Taylor and Hessey, Keats's publishers. Woodhouse made a transcription (now known as W^3) in William Taylor's shorthand that was used by the lawyers of the day, and then he made three separate longhand transcriptions of the poem from this shorthand version. Since one of these longhand transcriptions is missing, both the order and immediate sources of the surviving two copies, in two separate Woodhouse notebooks at Harvard—known as W^2 and W^1—are in doubt. Of these, W^1—probably the later of the two—contains a copy that Keats went over again. The text of the poem was changed by Woodhouse in W^3, the shorthand version, and further changed in the two derivative longhand transcripts; most of these changes were retained by Keats when he went over W^1, though the poet made some additional changes at this stage. Stillinger believes that W^1 was then given to John Taylor for publication and that Taylor made some further revisions in it before the poem went to the printer. These changes—like most of Woodhouse's and at least one early verbal change suggested by Reynolds and incorporated at an earlier stage—became part of the public poem in Keats's poetic volume of 1820, *Lamia, Isabella, The*

Eve of St. Agnes, and Other Poems, which also contains seven textual changes from the press-copy transcript.[31]

Rather than spending more time detailing such clear-cut cases of authors who can be shown to have authorized a cooperative program to revise and prepare their works for the public (instead of asking the printer and publisher simply to follow the manuscripts they originally submitted for publication), let us look again at Shelley, who seemed to resist as forcefully as any writer of his age interference by the men and the means of production. In attempting to publish *Laon and Cythna; or, The Revolution of the Golden City,* the twelve-book romance-epic that is Shelley's longest poem, Shelley himself selected the printer, Buchanan McMillan, and had at least part of *Laon and Cythna* set in type before he secured a bookseller to distribute the poem. McMillan's compositors presumably followed Shelley's explicit instructions not to emend anomalies.[32] Yet even in this case, collation of the surviving press copy with the first edition indicates clearly that Shelley expected the compositors to make a number of changes in order to present his work to the public.

For one thing, the orthography of the press-copy manuscript contains ampersands and other standard abbreviations ("w^d." for "would," "sh^d." for "should") that Shelley intended the printers to spell out in full. Similarly, the compositors corrected Shelley's misspellings to the conventional orthography—specially words containing the combination *ie* or *ei* (such as the possessive adjective *their,* which Shelley often, but not invariably, spelled "thier"). Either the compositors or Shelley, when reading proofs, capitalized the initial letters of some nouns (and less often removed such capitals) and modified the pointing in a number of places—adding commas, changing dashes to semicolons and other marks of punctuation, and adding or subtracting apostrophes to conform to current typographical practice. Shelley, like Coleridge, often included an apostrophe in the possessive adjective *its*—"it's"—a usage that was sanctioned by grammar books of the eighteenth century but had fallen from favor by 1817.

Lastly, McMillan's print shop regularized the typography.

In presenting the poem's Spenserian stanzas, the compositor changed Shelley's arabic numerals to small roman numerals for the stanzas of each canto and regularized the indentations that Shelley's holograph employs (sporadically) to mark the rhyme scheme, leaving only the ninth line of each stanza—the Alexandrine—extended to the left of the other eight lines. The pages were arranged in the standard pattern for poems with eight- or nine-line stanzas, with two stanzas on each page. The heading of each canto was printed in Gothic type. These and other matters of format, not indicated in Shelley's holograph, helped produce the bibliographic codes that identified Shelley's poem as a typical exotic romance of the period in ottava rima or Spenserian stanzas, the best-known of which was Byron's *Childe Harold's Pilgrimage*. The page layout, like Shelley's deceptive title, was clearly part of his plan to follow up the success of such romances—including preeminently Scott's and Byron's poems and Thomas Moore's *Lalla Rookh* (1817)—by disguising his revolutionary poem as one of the exotic adventure narratives currently popular with British readers.[33] Yet these patterns appear only sporadically, if at all, in the holograph. Shelley's intention was that the printer and (for the title page) his publisher would add elements to his manuscript version that would enable his private vision to circulate successfully in the public marketplace. Whether Shelley verbally instructed the printer in the forms he desired or McMillan's compositors added them according to the rules of their craft, the first printing provides a more authoritative copy-text than does the setting manuscript, which survives only in fragments anyway.

Surprisingly, the edition of Byron's works by Jerome J. McGann, one of the chief advocates of observing and crediting the social means of production as part of the authorial process, repeatedly removes such features originating at the press to return to presentational idiosyncrasies of Byron's manuscripts even in cases where Byron read proofs and clearly approved the changes therein instituted.[34] McGann's and Stillinger's editorial practices, like mine, have been so strongly influenced by the Greg-Bowers-Tanselle orthodoxy of the past thirty years that in the actual editing we have completed (as distinguished from our more recent theorizing about editing), we have only imperfectly aligned our practice with our emerging theories. We must admit this much before criticizing other editors for doing as we have done, rather than as we now say editors should do.

VI.
Summary

In concluding this discussion of the nature and proper uses of *private, confidential,* and *public* manuscripts, let me recapitulate some of the principal points that have been raised. Because manuscripts, unlike printed books, are unique, they represent the private world of the author's individual intentions more clearly than do printed books. Whereas books and other multiplied communications aspire to uniformity and, certain bibliographers argue, point toward an ideal archetype, the study of manuscripts bolsters humane appreciation of difference and individuality in an increasingly impersonal civilization, as scientific and statistical thinking and revolutions in industry and agriculture destroyed the nexus of long-term personal relations and loyalties characteristic of feudal societies.

Since the development of print publication, both the survival and the perceived importance of private manuscripts and confidential early drafts of public writings (especially literary works) have grown in direct proportion to the increased depersonalization of the social milieu. Thus, the Romantic interest in, and valorization of, the development of exceptional individuals can be identified as a reaction against such depersonalization and marks a reaffirmation of some humane ideals of the older social order. During the era of modern manuscripts, even those writers who were most opposed to the mechanical and impersonal aspects of modern society have expected the literary works they produced for the *public* to be multiplied and distributed by mechanical or electronic means; therefore, except in a few unusual cases, the hand-written or typewritten manuscripts that they send to the press do not represent their true *final* intentions, even for that particular moment.[35] Moreover, when authors publish revised versions of their works, the changes can often be seen, not as true changes of their intentions, but as attempts to restate the same intentions after an impersonal reading public has misinterpreted their first formulations.

Finally, the relatively recent wave of collecting, publishing, and analyzing *private* and *confidential* as well as traditional *public* manuscripts has produced problems for writers, editors, and readers that have not yet been fully addressed—especially when editors and publishers have failed to distinguish between these three distinct types. If editors persist in disregarding authors' intentions concerning the privileged status of their final or public texts, some writers may be tempted to destroy earlier versions of their works, just as some authors, responding to the misuse of private letters, have destroyed their personal papers lest they be misused.

In the concluding chapter, I attempt to show how the study of modern manuscripts and an understanding of the impetus for the study of *personal* or *private* manuscripts—a movement so strong that now the authors' own *public* texts are in danger of being undervalued or replaced—can be channeled into more positive directions if we envision all literary studies in more personal, less "scientific" terms. I outline a "personalist poetics" that can fulfill the obvious desire to free texts and readers from mechanistic subservience to mass production and other dehumanizing forces of modern industrial society, while honoring the respective claims and contributions to the artistic communication of the author, the social milieu, the inscribed text, and the reader.

MODERN MANUSCRIPTS AND

PERSONALIST POETICS

❖

Thus far, while showing how the distinctions between private, confidential, and public manuscripts can play a significant role in literary criticism, textual criticism, and editorial theory, I have also pointed to the importance of understanding both the intentions of authors and the nature of their intended audiences. Some literary and textual critics begin with a theoretical conception of a "text" or a "work" at the level of a Platonic ideal and then fail to distinguish between the authors' private drafts and their public texts. By positing ideal standards of communication that no author could live up to and then beginning to edit from an intermediate manuscript, for example, rather than from a text that the author saw through the press and approved, an editor may seek to elevate tinkering and cobbling to equality with the imaginative creativity of the originating author. Both deconstructive critics and idealizing editors who claim a share in unraveling or perfecting an unrecorded conception or "ideal" text ("the work") place burdens upon authors' imperfect means of transmitting their ideas that mere human beings and their artifacts should not be compelled to bear.

What may be needed is a human scale of values with which to measure the all-too-human activity of verbal communication. In this chapter, I shall use my ideas about the study of modern manuscripts to outline a program for literary studies—

or, rather, a governing metaphor to characterize literary studies—that both clarifies the relationships among the basic aspects of literary scholarship and criticism and keeps before us
all the important aspects of literary communication under a
single rubric based on normal human relationships, rather than
on some reification of theoretical goals. The conception,
though far from revolutionary in its consequences, claims the
virtue of focusing readers' attention on important distinctions
among the responsibilities of bibliographers and textual scholars, historical scholars, and literary critics, as well on as the
inevitable limitations of all the productions of mortal beings.
It grants every work of art its full share of autonomy, while
relating each poem or fiction both to its genetic heritage and
to its generic nature; at the same time, it gives weight to the
author's intentions for the work, the social forces that helped
determine its final shape, and its interactions with readers of
different times and places. I will not exaggerate the significance
of this conception by calling it a "metaliterary theory" or a
metaphysical system: it is merely a humane, comprehensive,
and practical program for ordering the priorities of efforts to
study any stage—or all stages—of any written communication
from an author to a specific reader or to readers in general.
This program I call *personalist poetics*.

I.
The Mind as Mother

I begin with a sonnet that Gerard Manley Hopkins sent to
Robert Bridges:

To R. B.

The fine delight that fathers thought; the strong
Spur, live and lancing like the blowpipe flame,
Breathes once and, quenchèd faster than it came,
Leaves yet the mind a mother of immortal song.

Nine months she then, nay years, nine years she long
Within her wears, bears, cares and combs the same:
The widow of an insight lost she lives, with aim
Now known and hand at work now never wrong.

Sweet fire the sire of muse, my soul needs this:
I want the rapture of an inspiration.
O then if in my lagging lines you miss

The roll, the rise, the carol, the creation,
My winter world, that scarcely breathes that bliss
Now, yields you, with some sighs, our explanation.[1]

Here the poet depicts his mind as a female whose womb, impregnated by "the fine delight that fathers thought," produces after a Horatian nine-year gestation an "immortal song."

In another sonnet of 1889, Hopkins uses a different image. Even as he admits that "Thou art indeed just, Lord," he raises the laments of both the Psalmist ("Why do sinners' ways prosper? and why must / Disappointment all I endeavor end?") and the unknown classical poet of the *Pervigilium Veneris:*

> See, banks and brakes
> Now leavèd how thick! lacèd they are again
> With fretty chervil, look, and fresh wind shakes
>
> Them; birds build—but not I build; no, but strain,
> Time's eunuch, and not breed one work that wakes.
> Mine, O thou lord of life, send my roots rain.

Although the poet mixes the springtime metaphors in the second sonnet, as he identifies himself with both the nesting birds and the renewed growth of the trees, this sonnet also maintains the overall metaphor of the poet as an adult giving birth to new life in the form of poems engendered by an outside prolific force, whether figured as God himself or as the delight of spirit that Hopkins would always attribute to God.

Hopkins's metaphors derive from others in the literary tradition.[2] Wordsworth's "Ode: Intimations of Immortality,"

Keats's "Ode to a Nightingale," and Shelley's *Adonais* draw
on the tradition of *Pervigilium Veneris,* in which the celebrant
of Venus's fecundity and power to rejuvenate nature ends by
lamenting that though he can see the joy of the bounding
lambs and mating birds, in the human world, "men sit and
hear each other moan, / Where palsy shakes a few, sad, last
grey hairs, / Where youth grows pale, and spectre-thin, and
dies; . . . ." At the end of his sonnet on King's College Chapel,
Wordsworth writes of "thoughts whose very sweetness yield-
eth proof / that they were born for immortality." In "Dejec-
tion: An Ode," Coleridge wrote of *his* loss of

> . . . Joy that ne'er was given,
> Save to the pure, and in their purest hour,
> Life and Life's effluence, cloud at once and show'r,
> Joy, Lady! is the spirit and the power,
> Which wedding Nature gives to us in dower
> A new Earth and new Heaven, . . .

The copulation of Psyche and Cupid in the first stanza of
Keats's "Ode to Psyche" represents the process of poetic inspiration and, hence—given Keats's strong veneration for poetry—of religious inspiration as well. And Tennyson, in section
85 of *In Memoriam,* had represented his "heart, tho' wid-
owed," as bringing that poem as an "imperfect gift" to his
dead friend:

> Ah, take the imperfect gift I bring,
>   Knowing the primrose yet is dear,
>   The primrose of the later year,
> As not unlike to that of Spring.

Hopkins's two sonnets combine these earlier elements, proclaiming that poetry is a gift of divine joy, engendering in the
human mind, which develops and in the fullness of time bears
the poetic creation.

Other writers have employed parallel metaphors not deriving from *Pervigilium Veneris* that also treat literary works as
living, organic creations. Dante and other poets of *il dolce stil
nuovo* addressed their poems, personified as the daughters of

joy or of sorrow, in envois as they sent the poems to their
friends or mistresses.[3] Milton in *Areopagitica* declares that
"books are not absolutely dead things, but do contain a po-
tency of life in them to be as active as that soul was whose
progeny they are. . . . a good book is the precious life-blood
of a master spirit, embalmed and treasured up on purpose to
a life beyond life."[4] Shelley, following such conventions in
Epipsychidion, addresses his poem as a daughter in the envoi:

> Weak Verses, go, kneel at your Sovereign's feet,
> And say: — "We are the masters of thy slave;
> What wouldest thou with us and ours and thine?"
> Then call your sisters from Oblivion's cave,
> All singing loud: "Love's very pain is sweet,
> But its reward is in the world divine
> Which, if not here, it builds beyond the grave."
> So shall ye live when I am there. Then haste
> Over the hearts of men, until ye meet
> Marina, Vanna, Primus, and the rest,
> And bid them love each other and be blest:
> And leave the troop which errs, and which reproves,
> And come and be my guest, — for I am Love's.[5]

Without explicating these lines in terms of the whole of *Epipsychidion,* let me stipulate that Shelley addresses this poem as
his youngest child and urges her and her sister poems to sing:
"Love's very pain is sweet, / But its reward" is in the divine
world that Love builds, if not in this world, then beyond the
grave. This immortal world is to be found in the very fact that
just as "when old age shall this generation waste," Keats's
Grecian Urn will say to new generations that "Beauty is Truth,
Truth Beauty," so these poems, daughters of Shelley's spirit,
"shall live" after the poet is "beyond the grave" and shall
continue to proclaim that "Love's very pain is sweet." The
basic metaphor found in these and related tropes is that the
poem is a living organism, fathered upon the psyche of the
poet by a powerful outside influence, brought to birth in the
world as the poet's mind has shaped it, and—if it proves to
be neither abortive nor ephemeral—living its life after its par-

ents, when the poet and the circumstances that inspired it are alive only in the memory of those who encounter this immortal progeny. If we take seriously the idea that the poem or novel or other freestanding work of art as conceived by the author and delivered into the world is a living being, with an identity of its own, what are the roles of scholar-critics who interest themselves in its welfare?

II.
The Editor as Physician

We may liken the editor of a text, depending at what stage he or she enters the case, either to an obstetrician, who helps to deliver as healthy a child as possible, or, if the birth has taken place before the editor reaches the scene, to a physician or surgeon, who helps repair the damage resulting from inadequate nutrition during gestation, trauma during childbirth, or childhood accidents. The authors' family members or friends who serve as their contemporary editors may be said to provide prenatal care and to assist with delivery of the poem or book, as Maxwell Perkins did for the novels of Thomas Wolfe, Ernest Hemingway, and F. Scott Fitzgerald. Among the Romantics, Percy Bysshe Shelley performed this office of obstetric editor for both *Frankenstein* and *History of a Six Weeks' Tour*, Mary Wollstonecraft Shelley's first two mature publications, before she returned the service for several of Shelley's works during his lifetime and then presented to the world many of his works that had not seen the light of day until she edited and published them either in *Posthumous Poems of Percy Bysshe Shelley* (1824)—among these, *The Witch of Atlas* and *Julian and Maddalo*—or in her two editions of *The Poetical Works of Percy Bysshe Shelley* that appeared in 1839, which included *Peter Bell the Third* and *Oedipus Tyrannus; or, Swellfoot the Tyrant*, to name only major, completed poems.

The initial editor, who may be a friend of the author but

is at least a contemporary, can assist with the prenatal care and help to deliver a complete and perfect work of art. Editors who helped bring Keats's poems to birth during his lifetime included Leigh Hunt (who also edited Shelley's *The Mask of Anarchy* for its emergence in 1832), Richard Woodhouse, John Taylor (who also edited many of the poems of John Clare before their first publication), and Charles Brown. After Keats's death, Richard Monckton Milnes (Lord Houghton) and Harry Buxton Forman brought forth other poems and fragments of Keats's work. For such assistance, Lord Byron depended first on his poet-kinsman Robert Charles Dallas and later on William Gifford (John Murray's editorial adviser), such friends as Thomas Moore, John Cam Hobhouse, and Douglas Kinnaird, and, in Italy, on Percy Bysshe Shelley's advice and the transcriptions of Mary W. Shelley, who copied several of his poems for the press and made suggestions and changes, the full extent of which has yet to be assessed. Among the Victorians, cooperative relationships between authors and literary advisers were common, especially when authors were not resident at the site of publication. Robert Louis Stevenson, for example, depended on his friend Sidney Colvin to act as literary agent and to shepherd to publication in England the stories he sent from Samoa.

But however well-meaning such editors-as-obstetricians may be, they (or the changed times in which a posthumously published work may emerge) can also mutilate the original conception of the author and misrepresent the times for which the work was originally intended. Mary Wollstonecraft died as the result of complications in giving birth to Mary Wollstonecraft Godwin (later Shelley); similarly, a potential literary masterpiece can be mutilated or even fatally damaged by an unskilled editorial physician, or even a relatively skilled one having a bad day. Recent textual analysis of the original manuscript of Stevenson's story "The Beach of Falesà," for example, suggests that Sidney Colvin, because of either his own prejudices or those of the British reading public, revised the text in such a way as to mute both Stevenson's criticism of the corrupt whites in Polynesia and his admiration of the native girl who saves the life of the white narrator to whom she was provided as a plaything.[6]

Byron, Shelley, and Keats all had reason to complain about the censorship performed on their poems. In "correcting" the poetry of John Clare, John Taylor canceled in the manuscripts some of Clare's most characteristic dialect diction of rural life because he considered it too "low" for poetry.[7] As time passed, the intellectual offspring of the Romantics fell into the hands of quacks and charlatans, who altered words and syntax because they were too lazy to read the passages carefully or to look words up in the dictionary to see what they meant, or who piously capitalized all of Shelley's references to God, even in passages where Shelley is declaring that if such a being as he described actually existed, the being would be, not God, but a demon.

Like human beings, the text of a work can suffer serious, repeated injuries and indignities without losing its identity or personality. Many of the poems of the Romantics emerged from the early twentieth century as famous and beloved works, even while bearing the scars of a hundred accidents and several misguided or unskilled attempts at cosmetic surgery. Although responsible modern textual scholars may arrive in time only to assess the damage attributable to such a series of mishaps, they may still be able to play an important role in restoring the poem or fiction to its intended state of health and beauty and thus in assuring it a long and happy life. These scholars first examine a text and gather as much information as possible about the conditions and events at the scene of birth and about the pediatric treatment it has received. They can thus evaluate the results of an author's failure to observe a proper prenatal regimen, discover mistakes by the attending physician or midwife, and note any removable birthmarks, scars, or impairments that can be safely remedied by corrective surgery.

Both contemporary and later editors must exercise caution in their work. Sometimes, as with Shelley's *The Mask of Anarchy* or *A Defence of Poetry*, delays in publication caused those who finally brought works to birth to "correct" parts that no longer seemed to them pertinent by the time the works appeared. But to image the Muse—the inspiration or occasion of the writing—as the inseminating force and the poet's mind as the womb in which the work of art grows suggests that to ignore a political event, such as the Peterloo Massacre, may not simply update the work but also disguise or deny one half of its parentage. In such cases, those who encounter the work in its later life are liable to misunderstand it simply because of their ignorance of half of its hereditary birthright. When a work has been thus mutilated at birth, the later textual scholar—aided by historical and biographical research—may simply need to identify the original state of the poem or essay and to restore those portions that may have been excised or altered by its initial editor, so that a swan will not be rejected as an ugly duckling.

When carrying out such restorations, editors must take care not to make wholesale changes just to show off their great power or sagacity. Occasionally, changes intended to be cosmetic merely follow the fashions of the editor's, rather than the author's, era. Bobbing a nose that current fashion deems too large—or modernizing the spelling and punctuation of a text—may result in both a loss of individuality and an aesthetic deprivation that at a still later time or a different place may be seen as hubristic butchery. (Those residing at Oxford are surrounded by the higher wisdom of the Victorian architects who "restored" or replaced Renaissance buildings with their own Gothic imitations.) Unless we are very careful, attempts to restore a work to the condition originally conceived by its author by undoing changes that occurred at its birth may be equally misguided.[8]

If we pursue the analogy that has been developed, without spinning it out to an extreme degree, the parallels hold reasonably well. The responsibilities of textual scholars thus include deciding not only *whether* but *how* to restore the work to the condition in which its author, inspired by the circumstances of the times, conceived and brought it into being. The prior decision whether to edit the work as it was finally published or as it was last approved by the author before it encountered the socializing process that brought it to birth is most crucial where a prepublication version of the work has been censored and altered before publication. In examining some of the issues involved, let us compare two celebrated cases of prepublication censorship: The earlier is Shakespeare's attempt to name the comic lead in *Henry IV, Part 1* Sir John Oldcastle until the playwright was (apparently) forced by pressure from Lord Cobham, a descendant of Oldcastle's, to change the name to Sir John Falstaff. The other instance is the censorship of Shelley's *Laon and Cythna*, in which the printer, Buchanan McMillan, and the publisher, Charles Ollier, forced Shelley to rename *The Revolt of Islam* and to cancel twenty-eight leaves, eliminating some derogatory references to Christianity and changing the relationship of the hero and heroine, who are lovers, from that of a blood brother and sister to that of a young man (Laon) and an orphan girl (Cythna) raised in his home.

In Shelley's case we know exactly how the text was changed and in what spirit the author acquiesced to the alterations. As we saw earlier, the press-copy manuscript of *Laon and Cythna; or, The Revolution of the Golden City* was a holograph that Shelley delivered to Buchanan McMillan, a printer selected by Shelley, and McMillan set at least part of the poem in type before booksellers were secured to distribute the poem.[9] In setting the text, McMillan's compositors, presumably observing Shelley's explicit instructions not to emend anomalies, followed his copy very faithfully. But once the poem was printed, either McMillan himself or some of the first readers of the poem—possibly some of Charles Ollier's customers among them—noticed that the plot took an advanced view of brother-sister incest and that orthodox religion came in for some harsh words. Both printer and publisher, who were in danger of legal action, demanded (especially in view of some recent trials of booksellers and printers for blasphemous libel) that Shelley revise his poem.[10] Thomas Love Peacock testifies that Shelley resisted all revisions at every step:

> Mr. Ollier positively refused to publish the poem as it was, and Shelley had no hope of another publisher. He

for a long time refused to alter a line: but his friends finally prevailed upon him to submit. Still he could not, or would not, sit down by himself to alter it, and the whole of the alterations were actually made in successive sittings of what I may call a literary committee. He contested the proposed alterations step by step: in the end, sometimes adopting, more frequently modifying, never originating, and always insisting that his poem was spoiled.[11]

In a marked copy of *The Revolt of Islam* that Shelley gave to friends in Italy, he continued to express unhappiness at the censorship of his poem, indicating that he remained dissatisfied with the published version.[12] On the basis of this and other evidence, a number of editors and textual critics have argued that Shelley's intention for *Laon and Cythna* was so badly thwarted by the censorship of the publisher and the printer that the modern editor should restore the text that Shelley fought so hard to maintain.

Further relevant facts of publication history make this decision to turn back the clock and undo the surgery performed at birth a viable one. The *Laon and Cythna* text had been neither lost nor totally sidetracked from literary history. A few copies of the original version had been distributed before the mutilation, including one that fell into the hands of the *Quarterly Review,* where it was attacked in one of the few widely read reviews of the poem. That review of his repressed and withdrawn poem, moreover, provoked Shelley to start an epistolary quarrel with Robert Southey, to satirize the Lake Poets in *Peter Bell the Third,* and to attack the *Quarterly* reviewers in both the preface and the text of *Adonais.*[13] Moreover, because the cancel leaves had not been substituted in the large stock of unbound sheets remaining from the overstock of unsold copies of *The Revolt of Islam,* a second issue of the poem sold in 1829, bound up with a new title page listing John Brooks as the publisher and *The Revolt of Islam* as the title, actually contained all the uncanceled sheets of the original printing of *Laon and Cythna.* Robert Browning (for one) later noted this difference between the received text and that of the first copy he had bought when he was a boy.[14] Thus, Shelley's preferred but suppressed text played an active part in the history of the poem's reception and reputation from the very first, and even before Harry Buxton Forman restored that text in his critically edited Library Edition of 1876, it had figured importantly in literary history.

The case of Oldcastle vs. Falstaff is not nearly as clear in its circumstances. We have neither documentary evidence nor eyewitness testimony, for example, about Shakespeare's intentions. If or when the censor came to him or to his acting company to ask that Oldcastle, a Lollard martyr, not be slandered by having his name associated with a charming but self-indulgent hedonist, was Shakespeare as reluctant to give a different name to his comic character in *Henry IV, Part 1* as Shelley was to alter his poem? In a provocative and cleverly sustained paper entitled "The Fortunes of Oldcastle," Gary Taylor has argued that for *Henry IV, Part 1* the editor should restore Shakespeare's original, uncensored version of the text by replacing the name Falstaff with that of Oldcastle in this play, though not in the succeeding plays—*Henry IV, Part 2, Henry V,* and *The Merry Wives of Windsor*—in which the name Falstaff was used from the start.[15] If one judges the evidence of this censorship to be convincing and then follows the rule of adhering strictly to authorial intention, trying to undo all interference of outside social constraints by recognizing as authoritative the last stage of creation in which the author wrote entirely according to his own, untrammeled creative freedom, one may well judge Oldcastle vs. Falstaff by the rule in Shelley's case.

Some problems arise, however, with the story of the censorship of Shakespeare's drama that are not present in that of Shelley's poem. First, most of the evidence for the existence of the earlier version and all the evidence on the reasons for the change of names would be classified as hearsay and deemed inadmissible in a court of law.[16] There is no sixteenth- or seventeenth-century manuscript or printed text, either extant or reported, that contains the putative "uncensored" version of the play. If Shakespeare was, in fact, forced to alter the name from Oldcastle, he may have decided that his freedom to develop the character of Falstaff apart from the associations evoked by Sir John Oldcastle's martyrdom far outweighed any loss to his original intention. Indeed, Shakespeare seems to have taken the name of Sir John Oldcastle, Lord Cobham, from an anonymous play entitled *The Famous Victories of Henry the Fifth* (ca. 1588), and in making this change, he seems also to have changed the names of two other companions of King Henry V in that play from Harvey and Russell to Bardolph and Peto. Thus, with or without the imposition of censorship from Sir William Brooke, the Lord Cobham of Shakespeare's day (who as Lord Chamberlain held a life-and-death grip on a playwright's future), Shakespeare seems to have opted for either less prominent or nonhistorical names for the disreputable companions of Prince Hal. Whatever Shakespeare's intentions may have been when he wrote *Henry IV, Part 1.* by the time he wrote *Henry IV, Part 2* and—by royal request—*The Merry Wives of Windsor,* the playwright had clearly ratified the use of the name Sir John Falstaff for the character, because neither he nor his company made any attempt to revive Oldcastle even after the Cobhams fell out of favor in court.[17]

The traditional arguments in support of retaining the name Falstaff rather than substituting (or restoring) Oldcastle are these: We know that Shakespeare accepted the name Falstaff, because he used this name from the start in three subsequent plays in which the same character appears. There is ample documentary evidence—including at least six quarto texts of *Henry IV, Part 1* published between 1597 and 1623 and the folio of that year—that the publicly approved name of the character was Falstaff. Not only have four centuries of subsequent theatrical and publishing history established the name Falstaff in the four plays by Shakespeare but the same period of historical study has established that Sir John Oldcastle was not an appropriate model for the character Falstaff as he evolved in that first play—a discrepancy that Shakespeare himself might have accepted, even without the threat of censorship. Approaching the editorial questions raised by the censorship of *Henry IV, Part 1* from the study of modern manuscripts, we can add two points. First, since the circulation of manuscripts among a small circle was still a normal mode of "publication" in the 1590s (*vide* Donne's poetry), had Shakespeare felt the need to establish a text of *Henry IV, Part 1* using the name Oldcastle, he had only to have friends copy and circulate such a text (e.g., from a prompt copy). Second, in the absence of such contrary evidence, the printing of "good" quartos in 1597/98 that not only use the name Falstaff in the text but feature it on the title page is sufficient to establish this version as the authorial one. Even the surfacing of a prompt copy of the play with Oldcastle's name would not show that this was Shakespeare's preference for his final *public* text, in the face of the whole of theatrical and publication history from 1598 to 1623.

On the more general issue of when an editor should try to undo contemporary censorship of the author's intentions, I would say that an editor should return to the readings of manuscripts or other authorially approved documents at those places where a previously accepted text can definitely be shown (on the basis of other contemporary evidence) to have been censored in ways the author continued to reject. But there is a serious danger in altering a text on the basis of a few fragments of contemporary evidence, linked by a web of conjecture, especially when to do so violates not only the organic integrity of the living work of literature but its friendships and associations with the large majority of its audiences. An editor espousing a personalist poetics will, of course, accord greater authority to the author than to readers in determining the text and meaning of a work, on the simple principle that it is absolutely impracticable, as well as inane, to take a child away from its surviving parent and raise it according to the will of the loudest or most nervy among ten thousand strangers. The personalist editor should, however, also have the good sense to recognize those instances in which the course of the child's growth and development supersedes parental influences of both nature and nurture combined.

The personalist scholar-critic, acting in the capacity of editor or textual critic, will try to balance the values inherent in the intentions of the author, the qualities of the work itself, and the sensibilities of its readers. As a citizen and human being, such a scholar-critic will have other values as well; he or she may not wish to seek to create the best text of *Mein Kampf,* for example. But once he or she has chosen to edit a work, the welfare of that poem, fiction, or treatise should demand and receive the textual scholar's best and most devoted efforts. Whether or not a personalist editor or textual critic decides to restore the work to its natal condition will frequently depend on casuistic factors in the history of the text and its reception rather than on some abstracted and theoretical rule. Among those who have a voice in that decision will be those who know and love the work as it has developed in literary history, though this need not prevent a personalist editor from making available alternative versions of the text (as has been done with the text of the Psalms by Benedictine scholars in their edition of the Vulgate Bible) so that readers in the future may acquaint themselves with the preferred scholarly text and come to love *that* version best.[18]

III.
The Historical Scholar as Biographer

In a personalist approach to literature, if editors and textual scholars can be regarded as physicians and surgeons, with varied specialties in obstetrics, pediatrics, and reconstructive surgery, how—retaining the same overall metaphor—shall we characterize scholars who study the historical and biographical backgrounds of a work? If we think of the work of art as an organic creation with its own personality and character, as well as its own life cycle, we might think of someone who probes into the background and circumstances of its birth and life as its *biographer.*

Historical researchers have two main lines of inquiry to pursue: the work's origins and its life history. Cooperatively, they seek to understand the genetic and environmental background of both "parents"—the artist whose mind gave birth to the work and the inspiriting experience, event, memory, emotion, or idea that led the author to bring forth the particular work. That "muse," or inseminating idea or occasion, may be as mundane as a fear of hunger or the need for rent money that makes an artist with writer's block suddenly produce a work after a long period of inactivity. But literary works that retain their value for several generations usually are stimulated by more profound sources. For example, it is often said that Dr. Johnson wrote his masterpiece *Rasselas* to earn enough money to pay the expenses of his mother's funeral. But surely it was the death of his mother—one of those existential crossings faced by all human beings—that provided such emotive force to the work. This seems clear when we consider its message. Prince Rasselas finds that all his roaming throughout the world can bring him no greater reward than did the Happy Valley of his birth and childhood. This nostalgia surely turns back to the image of the lost mother, as do many of the poems of Wordsworth, who had displaced the loss of his mother into a love of maternal Nature in the Lake Country, the Happy Valley of *his* childhood.

Scholarly biographers who study the family heritage of works of art often find that the ancestry is very complex. On the author's side there will be literally a collection of genes deriving from his or her own family's, as well as the author's personal reading, prior experiences, and the historical situation or individual circumstances that led him or her to encounter the engendering inspiration that produced the particular work. That inspiriting thought or event that provided the other side of the work's parentage might contain some of the same genetic material. *The Prelude,* for example, involves on the poet's side a specific family history and the growth of William Wordsworth's mind before he began to write that poem. This biography includes such private events as the early death of his parents and Wordsworth's later relations with his siblings and his adult guardians, but it also includes such public conditions as the educational curriculum at Cambridge at the end of the eighteenth century and the course of the French Revolution that made an impression on the poet, especially those that he witnessed firsthand or observed from a short distance. The other side of the poem's "family" includes some of that same historical material, since the disillusionment produced by the failure of Wordsworth's Enlightenment hopes, as these were dashed by his experience of the Reign of Terror, the Subjugation of Switzerland, and other public events, led to the changed values that inseminated his mind with this autobiographical impulse. (The parallels and interactions between the poet's private and public sorrows enabled him to embody his own losses and compensations in a narrative that came to epitomize the experience of the whole era.) The genealogy of *The Prelude* would also include, on both sides of the family, the Bible and writings by Plato, Descartes, Voltaire, Rousseau, and a large number of other poets and thinkers over the ages that influenced Wordsworth directly and also helped to shape both French and English society. The biographer of *The Prelude* cannot deal simply or neatly with such a varied yet melded genetic heritage but must probe deeply enough into the possible influences on both the author and the occasion to provide some sense of the complexities involved. Such a scholar will constantly be reminded—and will, in turn, remind other readers—that the work of art, like other living creatures, possesses a unique individuality exceeding the sum of its genetic origins and its experiences.

In addition to the heritage of a poem or novel on its first appearance, which includes its genetic inheritance from its author and its muse, as well as the care and nourishment the work received while it was gestating and during and after birth, each literary production also has a history of reactions by readers that help to shape its character. Each time a poem or novel encounters the world, like other living beings, it meets with a response from the "other" that helps to define and shape its "selfhood" and creates new parameters that, though not strictly determinative, affect its subsequent character and restrict its freedom by partially conditioning its future. Let me illustrate this point with an example from recent literature—

Allen Ginsberg's poem *Howl,* the manuscripts of which have recently been published in a single photofacsimile edition, together with early letters and reviews reacting to the poem.[19] This edition illustrates one side of modern self-consciousness about the preservation and use of manuscripts, for the author produces his own variorum edition (as Pope only pretended to do for satirical purposes with *The Dunciad*). It also provides other illustrations of the use and possible misuse of personal letters.

Jack Kerouac, Lucien Carr, William Carlos Williams, and the poet's father Louis Ginsberg (also a poet) all encouraged Allen Ginsberg's work on *Howl* after they read drafts of an early version typed by Robert Creeley and replicated in fifty copies by means of a Ditto machine. Ginsberg helped generate a favorable response for the poem from Richard Eberhart in a *New York Times* article on the San Francisco poetry scene by writing Eberhart a long, preemptive letter protesting Eberhart's earlier response to the poem in a conversation they had had in San Francisco; in that letter, Ginsberg explained both the poem's structure and its positive vision. Although Lionel Trilling (one of Ginsberg's teachers at Columbia) and Ezra Pound responded negatively in letters and although the success of the formal publication (October 1956), with a foreword by William Carlos Williams, was in doubt, enormous free publicity presented itself in March 1957 when the Collector of Customs in San Francisco seized 520 copies of *Howl and Other Poems* (printed in England by Villiers) on the grounds that it was an obscene publication. While the American Civil Liberties Union prepared to fight this seizure in the courts, Lawrence Ferlinghetti, the publisher-poet of City Lights Book Shop, had a new edition printed in America to keep the book out of the jurisdiction of the customs office. Although the book had not been reviewed by the mass media and although according to Ginsberg it was not for sale in New York bookstores, this legal ruckus paved its way to success.

By the time I bought my copy of the City Lights edition of *Howl,* Ginsberg had become a guru of the 1960s liberation and antiwar counterculture and the volume was in its twenty-first printing (of April 1969), with 186,000 copies already in print. The little paperback volume was touted on its back cover as having been "seized by the U. S. Customs and the San Francisco police" and having been defended by "a series of poets and professors [who] persuaded the court that the book was not obscene." Scholars unfamiliar with the milieu that brought this poem to prominence but wishing to understand the importance of *Howl* or Allen Ginsberg's importance in recent American poetry (or, for that matter, wishing to understand William Carlos Williams's place in the course of recent American literary history) would have to read such early correspondence, reviews, and the press notices of the legal proceedings concerning *Howl and Other Poems.* They would also have to study the literary interrelationships of the period—the westward migrations of the Beats and the Black Mountain poets, the San Francisco literary scene of the 1950s and early 1960s, and the neoromantic reaction against the poetics of Eliot and Pound, who, Ginsberg wrote to Trilling, were "like Dryden & Pope." From Ginsberg's comments, we learn that he considered Smart's *Jubilate Agno* and Shelley's *Adonais* and "Ode to the West Wind" as among the seminal sources for his poem.[20]

Many other works besides Ginsberg's *Howl* have won particularly strong initial responses during their early years— books of political or sociological impact (Burke's *Reflections on the Revolution in France* and Harriet Beecher Stowe's *Uncle Tom's Cabin*); literary efforts controversial for alleged aesthetic or moral reasons (Joyce's *Ulysses* or Salman Rushdie's *The Satanic Verses*); and books that changed the ideological or intellectual perspective of millions soon after their appearance (such as *The Communist Manifesto* or Darwin's *Origin of Species*). When a work develops an indelible reputation based on its reception, it is often difficult for it to be accepted by new readers on its own merits; like some controversial people, it may become a symbol of something larger and more abstract than its author conceived it to be. The Scopes trial in Tennessee for the teacher's right to teach the theory of evolution in the schools is merely one of the aftershocks generated by the symbolism arising out of Charles Darwin's books. And the number of mini-versions of the Scopes trial that in the United States have marked reactions of citizens to efforts to teach the works of Friedrich Engels and Karl Marx show how potent a symbolism remains in their publications. On the other hand, many books that caused a major stir at the time of their publication have now outgrown the fevered rhetoric that accompanied them into the world. Such works as Machiavelli's *The Prince* and Godwin's *Enquiry concerning Political Justice* are now read with much more detachment and attention to the intrinsic merits of their arguments, as logic and historical analysis replace the kind of rhetorical judgment that led Shakespeare's villainous Richard Crookback to wish to outdo "the murtherous Machevil." Not only did Godwin's work fail to remain a center of passionate controversy but during his own lifetime the author became almost a nonperson whose name even his disciple Shelley "had enrolled on the list of the honorable dead" as early as January 1812. By 1825, Hazlitt, admirer and friend of Godwin, wrote in *The Spirit of the Age* that Godwin, who "five-and-twenty years ago . . . was in the very zenith of a sultry and unwholesome popularity," has now "sunk below the horizon, and enjoys the serene twilight of a doubtful immortality."[21]

Some works of little value are brightened by the flames of controversy, while other, worthier ones are tarnished by its smoke. The history of both the meretricious fame and an undeserved neglect of a work—like the friendships and quarrels or rejections of an author—are important in the book's biography. They help shape its character, as that is perceived by each group of readers, for often a new generation will seek out and adopt a neglected or stigmatized author, work, or era to serve as its forebear. One duty of the personalist literary historian, in his role as biographer of the work, is to trace its course of life—the reactions of its readers of different times and places—to discover both what these reactions tell us about the original nature of the work and how the impact of these reactions may have modified that character. For example, does declaring a work canonical change its nature? Would *Julius Caesar* be a more important play in Shakespeare's *oeuvre* if students were not required to read it at the age of thirteen or fourteen? Would Spenser, on the other hand, be read at all if he were not anthologized for college surveys of English Renaissance literature and were he not on lists of required readings for English majors? And does this encounter of fragments of *The Fairie Queene,* read too fast and discussed inadequately in survey courses, explain why Spenser so seldom comes alive for the average undergraduate? These and other questions that relate to observable reader response, including the signs of influence and reaction from one writer or work to another, are in the province of the literary historian.

Historians of a living work of art have, then, much the same role as biographers of authors: first they trace the background and early development of the writing to learn about its essential characteristics; then they study the interactions of the literary work with the people, institutions, and ideological movements it has encountered either as friends or as enemies. The "biographer" of the work is naturally more concerned with the use of *private* and *confidential* documents than is the "physician"-editor. Whereas editors or textual critics examine all the drafts, intermediate transcripts, corrected proofs, and other way stations on the road to the finished work of art, their primary goal is to identify readings that the author intended to bring before the public but that were erroneously omitted or replaced during the process of transmission; the *editor* thus usually favors the final textual authorities. But the work's *biographer* relishes the unfinished and even rejected parts of the work in the drafts and revisions that may reveal more than the author intended to tell the public. Although the use by incautious editors of *private* letters or even of *confidential* drafts of poems or novels that the author meant to be seen only by intimate friends and trusted advisers has contaminated the texts of literary works edited upon principles of eclectic emendation, both the bio-historian of a work and the literary critic whose task is to introduce it to the public need just the kind of information that false starts and rejected drafts provide to measure the lines where fact and fiction merge and to delineate the principles that govern the author's artistic and ethical shaping of his materials.

IV.
The Critic as Family Friend

In a wide-ranging paper entitled "Textual and Literary Theory: Redrawing the Matrix," D. C. Greetham points out to students of bibliography and textual criticism the usefulness of becoming more keenly aware of current trends and issues in literary contemporary theory.[22] However, Greetham, perhaps for rhetorical effect, reverses the order of priority. As he notes, the discoveries of bibliographers and textual critics have proved invaluable to literary critics alert enough to seek them out; this advantage and priority inhere, I think, whether or not textual scholars have felt the need to attune their work to current fashions in literary theory. Much of the best such work—including the research and editing of Pollard, McKerrow, and Greg on Renaissance drama and that of R. W. Chapman on Jane Austen's texts—was carried out in defiance of the critical fashions of the day, and literary theorists updated their own work over the years as they absorbed and made use of the editorial discoveries.

But my conception of the relationship between textual and literary studies and theory may also differ from the views of some textual scholars and bibliographers, because I consider myself first and foremost a scholarly critic of literature who uses bibliographical and textual studies as means to comprehend poems and poetic dramas. Beginning with an analysis of Shelley's "The Triumph of Life" and continuing into my study of works from "The Clerk's Tale" of Chaucer and Shakespeare's *Richard II* to the novellas of Henry James and the poems of A. R. Ammons, my experience has been that bibliographical analysis and textual criticism help me achieve a richer literary understanding than I could have aspired to without their aid. When someone else had done the textual work (as is the case for Chaucer and Shakespeare), a critic may need only to study the arguments about the significance of the textual evidence for their analyses. But with more recent literature—including the poetry of Shelley and Ammons—such work frequently had not yet been thoroughly done, and I felt obliged to look more than cursorily at the relations between primary textual authorities to see what they might reveal about the development of the author's intentions and to explore the problems of structure and language that the comparison of various versions can most readily reveal.

Though bibliographical and textual studies are fundamental to full comprehension of any literary work, bibliographical scholars should—as Greetham urges—acquaint themselves with current trends in literary studies for the same reason that biochemists who study human nutrition should monitor developments in medical education, so that their valuable contributions to human welfare will not be overlooked because of the ignorance of the practitioners who transmit such discoveries to a larger public. The value of bibliographical research might find wider recognition if those of us engaged in it would carry on educational campaigns to point out the implications of our work. Perhaps the late Fredson T. Bowers contributed so greatly to bibliographical studies because he was unwilling to build his better mousetrap and then wait for the world to beat a path to his door. Instead, through vigorous proselytizing and lobbying he won for bibliographical studies and critical editing the same recognition that historical scholarship and literary criticism enjoyed somewhat earlier.

Having examined the role of the textual critic-editor and the literary historian—family physician-surgeon and biographer, respectively—in a personalist program of aesthetics and literary studies, under which the literary work is accorded the status of a living organism, let us now turn to the role of the literary critic per se. In an early essay, I distinguished literary "scholarship" from "criticism" in these words:

> Literary *scholarship* should aid the teacher and student in understanding what a work of art did mean or should have meant to the sensitive reader at the time of its composition. . . .
> *Criticism,* on the other hand, should aid the teacher and student in ascertaining what the work of art amounts to in the present tense. Criticism must always be in the

first person singular or the imperative. It is a normative act. . . . Once the objective creation has been identified through careful analysis of its words, structure, and ideas, the critic must then determine the value of the experience of the work of art for the living man [or woman] who re-experiences it. . . .

Literature is a human product, having relevance only to human beings: without the author and his imaginative soul, the work of art cannot exist at all. . . ; without the reader, . . . the poem is uncreated, becoming mere marks on paper or stone that await reanimation by a sensitive human soul.[23]

In a personalist criticism, the *critic,* whose role it is to introduce and commend to less experienced readers works that the critic believes to be either personally or socially valuable, stands in the relation of an old *family friend* both to the work he or she speaks about and to the relatively small community in which the critic resides. That community of readers of belles-lettres was a small one in the days of Aristotle, Horace, Dryden, and Pope. For about a century and a half, from the 1780s to the 1930s, the audience for literary criticism became much larger, as the rapid growth of literacy and leisure time dramatically expanded the reading public in the vernacular languages. The new readers of literature often lacked the proper educational background, or were at least unsure of their capacity to understand the books that they were encountering for the first time, and they listened, therefore, to such critics as Johnson, Hunt, Hazlitt, Arnold, Sainte-Beuve, Gosse, Chesterton, Edmund Wilson, Leavis, and Trilling, even elevating them to positions of social influence. But since the advent of talking films and television, the popular market for literary arts has been progressively siphoned off, and the rise of artistic cinema has made further inroads, even among intellectuals, in the influence of letters. Though the *number* of readers of good books is now larger than in the time of Dickens and Tennyson, literary critics now lack influence in society, because many who can be classed as serious readers consider themselves to be as knowledgeable about what they read as most of those who earn a living as critics.

The critics with cultural and political influence are now commentators on the mass media, who reach the larger audience still willing to follow professional advice. Many more readers in America and Canada today are influenced by the comments of Alistair Cooke, the host the Public Broadcasting System's "Masterpiece Theater," than by any critic writing in the print media.[24] The five thousand, ten thousand, or twenty thousand readers of literary criticism, many of whom are themselves professional teachers of literature, constitute the small town in which critics, friends of their families, introduce kinfolk of some leading writers in that community—Sam Coleridge's youngest son *On the Constitution of Church and State,* Alex Pope's rambunctious boy *Dunciad* (the one who needed all those expensive operations), David Lodge's facetious daughter *Small World,* or old man Alighieri's oldest girl, *La Vita Nuova.* (It is amazing how some folks age so gracefully, when most of their contemporaries are long dead.)

To be more serious for a minute (though, as Horace and his followers say, literary studies should have sweetness as well as light), a critic who is worth reading or listening to will be one who knows well both the family of the literary work and the social circle into which the work is to be introduced or vindicated. C. S. Lewis played the role of critic to perfection in his essay "Shelley, Dryden, and Mr. Eliot" (1939) when he defended Shelley's poetry and criticized Dryden's against the opinions of T. S. Eliot in his Norton Lectures on *The Use of Poetry and the Use of Criticism.* Eliot had attacked Shelley as being not in tune with Christian doctrine or the classics.[25] Lewis, writing for those who regarded him as a more authoritative Anglican apologist and classicist than Eliot, defended Shelley by asserting that his poetry showed him to have been a better classicist and a more spiritual poet in the Dantesque tradition than Dryden had been. Eliot and others in the 1930s had attacked Shelley's *Alastor* as advocating a wasteful search for an impossible dream; Lewis did not break scholarly ground by showing that the poem actually warns readers *against* such self-indulgence, but he effectively defended a friend whose faults had been criticized by pointing out his good qualities:

> *Alastor* is a poem perfectly true to itself. The theme is universally interesting—the quest for ideal love. And both the theme and the treatment are fully suited to Shelley's powers. Hence the poem has an apparent ease, a noble obviousness, which deceives some readers. Mr. Eliot himself is too experienced a writer to be guilty of the delusion that he could write like Shelley if he chose; but I think many of Mr. Eliot's readers may suffer from it. . . . Of course it [*Alastor*] has its faults—some of the scenery is over-written, and the form of the line which ends with two long monosyllables comes too often. But these are not the sort of defects that kill a poem: the energy of imagination, which supports so lofty, remote, and lonely an emotion almost without a false note for seven hundred lines remains; and it deserves to be admired, if in no higher way, at least as we admire a great suspension-bridge. I address myself, of course, only to those who are prepared, by toleration of the theme, to let the poem have a fair hearing. For those who are not, we can only say that they may doubtless be very worthy people, but they have no place in the European tradition.[26]

Drawing upon Eliot's reverence for Dante, Lewis went on to say:

> Dante is eminently the poet of beatitude. He has not only no rival, but none second to him. But if we were asked to name the poet who most nearly deserved this inaccessible *proxime accessit,* I should name Shelley. Indeed, my claim for Shelley might be represented by the proposition that Shelley and Milton are, each, the half of Dante. . . . To be thus half of Dante . . . is fame enough for any poet. And Shelley, I contend, reaches this height in the fourth act of *Prometheus.*[27]

Although I have merely sampled Lewis's argument, it should be obvious that he carried out his defense as a friend of the family who had known Shelley's offspring for a long time, was aware of their past associations, and understood their parental heritage. He did not undertake original scholarship, either in textual criticism or in historical or biographical research on Shelley, though he had obviously read and thought about Shelley and his writings for many years and had absorbed the main scholarly information available in the 1930s. The same was true of Frederick A. Pottle, of Yale, whose essay "The Case of Shelley" was published in 1952 after attacks on Shelley by Eliot and other modernist writers, by Leavis and the Scrutineers, and by the Fugitive-Southern Agrarian New Critics, just then completing their Great Trek from Tennessee and Louisiana to Gambier, Ohio, Minneapolis, and New Haven.[28] Pottle helped to maintain an audience for Shelley among younger teachers, just as Shelley was on the verge of being drummed out of the university English curriculum in America. Pottle's motivation became clear to me after he wrote, in response to his election as an honorary member of the Keats-Shelley Association of America in 1980, that he had gone into English studies because of Shelley.

I don't know whether I have ever printed the story of my capture by Shelley. My undergraduate major was chemistry and did not contain a single course in English literature. I did a good deal of debating and public speaking, and far along in my senior year went to a Romantic anthology of my roommate's to try to pick up a quotation (I forget what it was) that I wanted to use. I opened to the Shelley section—and read straight through it. Next day I got the complete poems of Shelley and read straight through that. My life was changed. I no longer saw myself as a teacher of chemistry (which is probably what I would have ended as) but as a writer, a poet. I went into the Army soon afterwards and was sent to France and Germany, but all through my army service read and wrote with the idea of being an author. I decided I had better get some training in English literature, went to Yale and fell in love with scholarship within a month. I am still very grateful to the chemistry, which gave me useful grounding in science, but the encounter with Shelley came at just the right time for me. A literary gent was certainly what I was cut out for, not a scientist.[29]

Having experienced such a dramatic conversion and then having written his dissertation on Browning and Shelley, Pottle valued his friendship with Shelley's poems even after his own scholarly work had been recentered on the Boswell papers at Yale. He regularly taught the Romantics, and he wrote his few essays on Shelley based on his general understanding of the poetry and the poet rather than on detailed original research. Because Pottle did not have a vested professional interest in Shelley's current reputation, his witness to the virtues of those poems was all the more effective. He encouraged his students to undertake serious work on Blake, Coleridge, Byron, and Shelley—the out-of-fashion Romantics of the 1940s and 1950s—and thus played a major, if indirect, part in the revival of scholarly and critical interest in these writers in the 1960s, a revival spearheaded in North America by such scholar-critics as Marchand, Coburn, Erdman, Cameron, Frye, and Wasserman but seconded by many of Pottle's advisees, including Harold Bloom, Thomas McFarland, George Ridenour, E. D. Hirsch, Jr., and Jerome J. McGann.

As valuable as have been the contributions of academic critics who write intelligently for their colleagues on works and writers whom they love but on whom they have not carried out extensive research, specialist scholars can contribute even more when they turn from addressing their fellow scholar-teachers to writing more broadly focused essays that transmit their intimate knowledge of the individual qualities of the writers and works to a larger readership. Just as bibliographical knowledge will be integrated more rapidly into literary criticism if bibliographers preach to the unconverted, so literary criticism will reflect the state-of-the-art thinking of textual and historical scholars if these experts, the best friends of the works and writers under discussion, make known their latest advances to nonspecialist critics through lectures, review essays on recent criticism, or original critical contributions to publications that reach beyond the circle of other specialists or close friends to the broader literary community.

V.

A Theory against Theories

In closing, I return to the study of modern manuscripts to relate that discipline to the program of *personalist poetics* adumbrated in this chapter. The study of modern manuscripts is the study of the particular and the individual. No two modern manuscripts are exactly alike, nor in most instances are they expected to be. Not even carbon copies prove to be identical, and until the widespread use of photographic and xerographic copying, there were few virtually exact duplicates of any draft, intermediate fair copy, or press-copy transcription of literary works and few totally identical copies even of legal or official diplomatic documents. As theorists have maintained for centuries, literature presents unique instances and examples that somehow convey universal lessons; this emphasis on the unique particularity of human experience, so central to both the student of history and the literary artist, is always threatened in scholarship and criticism by the desire to turn the humanistic studies into sciences.

Both *scholarship,* the attempt to understand the literary work as its author wished it to be viewed by his or her intended contemporary audience, and *criticism,* the evaluation of the work's relevance to audiences of other times, places, or cultures, tend to generalize themselves into systems of universal or repetitive structures and patterns. But by disciplining ourselves through research with holograph manuscripts, the unique formative materials of literature, and by developing our individual "theories against theories," we can avoid being steamrollered by abstract systems that turn unique literary works into two-dimensional patterns.

Studying literary manuscripts is a good way to develop habits of mind congenial to the individuality of the creative process, particularly as that process works to produce poems and prose fictions, because while tracing the signs of the creative act from its first tentative drafts, in a unique handwriting, through its various stages of accretion, excision, and revision, until the work of art has been shaped to aesthetic fulfillment, we concentrate, not on the usual or typical—the realm of "regularization" and "normalization" presided over by copyeditors and censors—but on the unique and particular steps by which a writer transforms an idea or image into a communicative work in a particular genre by observing the general rules of grammar, syntax, and logic, while at the same time twisting and extending the capacities of language into new and stimulating shapes.

Normal expository prose introduces young people to the standard, accumulated wisdom of the past, just as the mechanical printing processes of the Gutenberg Galaxy aspire to exact replication of a normal, standard text, while seeking to obliterate the eccentric and the unique. For this reason, the perspective of those studying the unique manuscripts produced during the modern era will tend to bring readers closer to poets and writers of fiction than will the study of printed books. The original poet or novelist—one whose works break new ground for other writers and remain of lasting value to readers of various times and places—does not pretend to formulate universal laws, and the most valuable parts of such a creative writer's experience, thought, and language are those touches that are beyond the easy reach of other human beings, elements that are neither standardized nor typical. Creative writers begin with the ordinary tools of communication but transform them into vehicles that can introduce other human beings both to new experiences and to higher levels of understanding. In a personalist program of literary studies, the particular work of art is seen as a unique entity that can be understood and related to by its author, by its readers, and by other authors and works. It cannot simply be categorized or subverted by any single typology, taxonomy, or system.

Whether or not such a program can be seen as a comprehensive way to approach all communications between authors and readers through the written word, such a humanistic poetics may at least prove to be a useful corrective to the excesses of more abstractly theoretical systems in an already overconventionalized and regimented society.

NOTES

❖

PREFACE

1. D[avid] C. Greetham, *Textual Scholarship: An Introduction* (New York: Garland Publishing, 1992), p. x.

CHAPTER ONE
INTRODUCTION: MODERN MANUSCRIPTS

1. The chief exceptions to this generalization that come to mind, such as the use of clay tablets in early Mesopotamian cultures, do not belong to the modern era.

2. Among many relevant studies by these authors, I note particularly Northrop Frye, *A Study of English Romanticism* (New York: Random House, 1968; repr., Chicago: University of Chicago Press, 1982); Morse Peckham, *The Birth of Romanticism* (Greenwood, Fla.: Penkevill Publishing, 1986); M. H. Abrams, *Natural Supernaturalism: Tradition and Revolution in Romantic Literature* (New York: W. W. Norton, 1971); Marilyn Butler, *Romantics, Rebels, and Reactionaries* (Oxford: Oxford University Press, 1981); and Jonathan Wordsworth, Michael C. Jaye, and Robert Woof, *William Wordsworth and the Age of English Romanticism* (New Brunswick, N.J.: Rutgers University Press, 1987).

3. Donald H. Reiman, *Intervals of Inspiration: The Skeptical Tradition and the Psychology of Romanticism* (Greenwood, Fla.: Penkevill Publishing, 1988).

4. The undertext of this palimpsest in the Vatican was first discovered by Angelo Mai in 1819 (see L. D. Reynolds's summary account in *Texts and Transmission: A Survey of the Latin Classics*, ed. L. D. Reynolds [Oxford: Clarendon Press, 1983; corrected repr., 1986], pp. 131–32).

5. Elizabeth L. Eisenstein notes in her Hanes Lecture *Print Culture and Enlightenment Thought* (Chapel Hill: Rare Book Collection/

University of North Carolina Library, 1986): "In the age of scribes, men of learning had served primarily as transmitters of an inherited corpus of texts. . . . After printing, less effort was required to preserve and pass on what was known; more energy could be spent on exploration and investigation" (p. 6).

6. Peter Abelard is a test case, for both many of his letters and his autobiography do survive. But Abelard, whose doctrines were proto-Enlightenment views, fought with all his orthodox contemporaries, and one reason for preserving and transmitting his life story may have been to show how personal sins lead to false doctrines.

7. Elizabeth Gaskell, *Cranford,* with a preface by Anne Thackeray Ritchie (London: Macmillan & Co., 1891), pp. 75–91. In chapter 8, Matty speaks of her "regular time for looking over the last week's bills, and notes, and letters, and making candle-lighters of them" (p. 133). In Jane Austen's *Persuasion,* when Anne Elliot reads an insult to her father in a private letter that she is being shown by someone trying to protect her family, "she was obliged to recollect that her seeing of the letter was a violation of the laws of honour, that no one ought to be judged or be known by such testimonies, that no private correspondence could bear the eye of others" (*Persuasion,* p. 204, in volume 5 of *The Novels of Jane Austen,* ed. R. W. Chapman [Oxford: Clarendon Press, 1926]).

8. Godwin undertook major revisions of *Of Population,* published in 1820 (see *Shelley and his Circle,* vol. 8, ed. Donald H. Reiman [Cambridge: Harvard University Press, 1986], pp. 969–76).

9. There is extant in the Pierpont Morgan Library an important holograph of a prose work by Sidney. The revised intermediate holograph of his *Defence of the Earl of Leicester* (his uncle, whose military leadership had been attacked) was written shortly before the author's tragic death in the Low Countries; it might, therefore, have been kept as a kind of relic, even after scribal copies had been circulated among his family and friends.

10. *Autograph Poetry in English: Facsimiles of Original Manuscripts from the Fourteenth to the Twentieth Century,* comp. and ed. P. J. Croft, 2 vols. (New York: McGraw-Hill Book Co., 1973), 1:xv–xvi.

11. Richard Hooker, *Of the Laws of Ecclesiastical Polity: Book V,* ed. W. Speed Hill (Cambridge: Harvard University Press, 1977), p. xv.

12. W. Speed Hill's comments on the rarity of such holograph

press copies may be compared with T. H. Howard-Hill's discussion of the unusual case of Middleton's *Game at Chess,* in which the author, to disseminate the play after it was suppressed by the Privy Council because of its bold political satire in the first production late in 1624, wrote out at least two complete copies of the drama (one of which served as press copy) and contributed to at least two more of "at least thirteen copies of the play . . . made in the six months or so between the performance and publication." The very unusual circumstances led the author to play an unusual role in the textual transmission (see "The Author as Scribe or Reviser? Middleton's Intentions in *A Game at Chess,*" *TEXT: Transactions of the Society for Textual Scholarship* 3 [1987]: 305–18). Middleton's activities provide a concrete example in England of a phenomenon Elizabeth L. Eisenstein has noted on the Continent in the eighteenth century, namely, that though "the continued circulation of hand-copied books is sometimes regarded as being incompatible with resort to the printed word, the two could work together to the disadvantage of censors and officials" (*Print Culture and Enlightenment Thought,* p. 19).

13. In *Medieval Scribes, Manuscripts, and Libraries: Essays Presented to N. P. Ker,* ed. M. B. Parkes and Andrew G. Watson (London: Scolar Press, 1978), 117–42.

14. Editors of Renaissance drama have much to say about plays being printed from "foul papers," but I have been unable to ascertain exactly how many such drafts or revised fair copies survive for their inspection. Even if, as Ben Jonson advocated, some authors did blot many lines, most of these authors or their heirs either destroyed the evidence of their false starts or at least considered these to be of so little value that they made no effort to preserve them.

15. The physician and professor of medicine Geronimo (or Girolamo) Cardano (1501–76), for example, wrote a Latin autobiography *De Vita Propria Liber* in 1574. At about the same time, the English music master Thomas Whythorne also wrote one (see James M. Osborn, *The Beginnings of Autobiography in England* [Los Angeles: Clark Library, 1960] and his edition of *The Autobiography of Thomas Whythorne* [Oxford: Clarendon Press, 1961]).

16. Iris Origo, *Images and Shadows: Part of a Life* (New York: Harcourt Brace Jovanovitch, 1970), pp. 189–90. Origo's book on Datini, *The Merchant of Prato, Francesco di Marco Datini* (New York: Alfred A. Knopf, 1957), gives the human story derived from these manuscripts.

17. *A Seventeenth-Century Letter-Book: A Facsimile Edition of Folger MS. V.a.321*, transcript, annotation, and commentary by A. R. Braunmuller (Newark: University of Delaware Press, 1983).

18. A similar function may be posited for a more unified English Renaissance letterbook containing scribal copies of twenty-six of Bacon's letters between 1595 and 1621 that deal with his governmental career and official business; it may have been compiled as a career guide for an aspiring public official (see Kenneth A. Lohf, "A Manuscript of Sir Francis Bacon's State Papers and Letters," *Columbia Library Columns* 38 [February 1989]: 30–32).

19. *The Correspondence of Sir Richard Steele*, ed. Rae Blanchard (London: Oxford University Press and Humphrey Milford, 1941); *The Book of Abigail and John: Selected Letters of the Adams Family, 1762–1784*, ed. L. H. Butterfield, Marc Friedlander, and Mary-Jo Kline (Cambridge: Harvard University Press, 1975).

20. *Diary and Autobiography of John Adams*, ed. L. H. Butterfield, Leonard C. Faber, and Wendell D. Garnett (Cambridge: Harvard University Press, 1961), p. xiii.

21. Ibid., p. xiv. According to a later appraisal by Richard Alan Ryerson, Butterfield's successor as editor in chief of the Adams Papers, "Taken together, the Adams diaries, letterbooks, loose letters, and miscellaneous items total about 300,000 manuscript pages" (see "Editing a Family Legacy: The Adamses and Their Papers," *Documentary Editing* 11 [September 1989]: 57).

22. *Literary Research* 13 (Fall 1988): 213–17.

23. *New York Times*, 27 March 1989, p. C13.

24. Of course the dates I give for the period between manuscript dearth and manuscript glut are almost arbitrary, but in Peter Beal's *Index of Literary Manuscripts, Vol. II: 1625–1700, Part I, Behn-King* (London: Mansell Publishing, 1987), the earliest poet whose autographs survive in quantity is Samuel Butler (1612–80), and the prose writers with the richest collections are Thomas Hobbes (1588–1679), Edward Hyde, first earl of Clarendon (1609–74), and John Evelyn (1620–1706). At a sale of manuscripts at Sotheby's in London on 15 December 1988, fourteen of the sixteen surviving letters of the poet Robert Herrick (1591–1674) came to sale in a single lot from the papers of his uncle Sir William Herrick (d. 1653) and are now in the Bodleian.

CHAPTER TWO

INTEREST IN THE PERSONAL AND THE
COLLECTING OF MANUSCRIPTS

1. The career of Thomas, Cardinal Wolsey (?1475–1530), reputedly the son of a butcher who rose to be lord chancellor of England, provides an epitomizing example of this mobility.

2. On the breakdown of the older Greek values see E. R. Dodds, *The Greeks and the Irrational* (Berkeley and Los Angeles: University of California Press, 1951). For the disintegration of traditional Roman values and the resemblances between the intellectual and social situations in the Hellenistic and late Roman Republican periods, on the one hand, and that facing the English Romantics, on the other hand, see Reiman, *Intervals of Inspiration,* esp. chaps. 1 and 6.

3. The deleterious effects on Wollstonecraft's reputation of the publication of Godwin's *Memoirs of the Author of the Vindication of the Rights of Woman* can be seen most dramatically, perhaps, in the course of her early reputation in America (see Marcelle Thiébaux, "Mary Wollstonecraft in Federalist America," in *The Evidence of the Imagination,* ed. D. H. Reiman, M. C. Jaye, and B. T. Bennett [New York: New York University Press, 1978], pp. 195–235). For the effect of the reaction on Godwin himself see William St. Clair, *The Godwins and the Shelleys* (New York: W. W. Norton & Co., 1989), esp. chaps. 14 and 15.

4. *The Letters of Percy Bysshe Shelley,* ed. Frederick L. Jones, 2 vols. (Oxford: Clarendon Press, 1964), 1:242; hereafter cited as "Shelley, *Letters.*"

5. *Posthumous Poems of Percy Bysshe Shelley* [ed. Mary W. Shelley] (London: John & Henry L. Hunt, 1824), p. viii.

6. *The Poetical Works of Percy Bysshe Shelley,* ed. Mrs. Shelley [1 vol.] (London: Edward Moxon, 1840), p. xi. Mary Shelley's first edition of Shelley's poetry was *The Poetical Works of Percy Bysshe Shelley,* ed. Mrs. Shelley, 4 vols. (London: Edward Moxon, 1839).

7. *Essays, Letters from Abroad, Translations, and Fragments,* 2 vols. (London: Edward Moxon, 1840) 1:vi–vii. For some unstated reason, Mary Shelley did not choose to reprint any of the early philosophical and political tracts that Shelley himself had published.

8. On John Palmer (1742–1818) see the *Dictionary of National Biography (DNB).*

9. *Memoirs of the Life and Writings of William Hayley, Esq., The Friend and Biographer of Cowper, Written by Himself . . . ,* ed. John

Johnson, 2 vols. (London: Henry Colburn and Simpkin & Marshall, 1823).

10. Although there were literally thousands of such attempts, it will suffice here to mention Coleridge's *Biographia Literaria,* the Shelleys' *History of a Six Weeks' Tour,* De Quincey's *Confessions of an English Opium Eater,* Hazlitt's *The Spirit of the Age,* and Carlyle's *Sartor Resartus.* Later in the nineteenth century, amid Victorian restrictions on the confessional mode, such well-known professional writers as Dickens, Mark Twain, and Henry James earned money from travel books with a personal focus when their movements made it difficult for them to keep to a schedule of more creative work.

11. An early annual that provided portraits along with biographical information was Sir Richard Phillips's series entitled *Public Characters.* The first volume, *Public Characters of 1799–1800* (1799) featured a foldout engraved frontispiece containing bust-length portraits of twenty-four (including Cowper, Sheridan, Mrs. Inchbald, and the countess of Derby) of the forty-seven whose biographies were included. By the ninth volume (1807), the frontispiece portrayed only Lord Somerville and the admiral Lord Collingwood. Michael Sadlier traces the degeneration of this fad in the later gift-book "annuals" while describing Lady Blessington's work as editor of Heath's *The Book of Beauty* (see Sadlier, *The Strange Life of Lady Blessington* [New York: Farrar, Straus & Co., 1947], pp. 179–85).

12. In addition to the comprehensive three-volume *Finden's Illustrations of the Life and Works of Lord Byron* (London: John Murray & Charles Tilt, 1833), there were a number of smaller series of illustrations, such as *The Byron Gallery; A Series of Historical Embellishments to Illustrate the Poetical Works of Lord Byron* (London: Smith, Elder & Co., 1833).

13. Charles Richard Sanders, *Carlyle's Friendships and Other Studies* (Durham, N.C.: Duke University Press, 1977), p. 77. In our day, when the demand for memorabilia of famous strangers has increased beyond the power of mere human beings to supply, mass-produced photographs have superseded locks of hair, and signatures of celebrities are manufactured by writing machines. Thus technological "progress" in modern society has again thwarted attempts to personalize and humanize experience.

14. See Thomas Hardy, *The Life and Work of Thomas Hardy,* ed. Michael Millgate (Athens: University of Georgia Press, 1985).

15. *Times Literary Supplement (TLS),* 11–17 August 1989, p. 864.

16. H. R. Woudhuysen observed in a piece on Dawson Turner in *TLS* (27 July–2 August 1990, p. 800) that besides his collections of autographs—begun about 1815, sold at auction in 1859, "and now scattered"—"Turner's own correspondence was extensive: Trinity College, Cambridge, alone has over 16,000 letters bound in eighty-two volumes and one witness saw a further seventy or so volumes at his home in 1853." On Turner, William Upcott (1779–1845), and the overall subject see A. N. L. Munby, *The Cult of the Autograph Letter in England* (London: Athlone Press, 1962). For the history of Sir Thomas Phillipps's collection and its final dispersal see Munby's five "Phillipps Studies," published by Cambridge University Press between 1951 and 1960.

17. Throughout the later eighteenth and the nineteenth century, and even well into the twentieth century, such British gentlemen as these would purchase or barter for Greek, Latin, Italian, and French manuscripts in large quantities and might sell, disperse, or donate them. An imaginative lawyer named James P. R. Lyell bequeathed one hundred manuscripts to the Bodleian Library and ordered the rest of his collection sold at auction, from the proceeds of which there was endowed a lectureship in bibliography. These men are known in the *DNB* and similar reference books as "antiquarians," "bibliophiles," or "philanthropists."

In the latter half of the nineteenth century, wealthy Americans with a cultural turn—such as J. Pierpont Morgan and his son "Jack" Morgan, Henry Clay Folger, and Henry E. Huntington—began to acquire similar collections of books and manuscripts, buying parts of the British collections of classical and Continental manuscripts that came on the market but more often concentrating on areas of English literary history that had not been as assiduously collected in Britain. They were known in British bookish circles as "robber barons" and "*nouveaux riches* collectors."

18. Gordon Ray, *Books as a Way of Life,* ed. G. Thomas Tanselle (New York: Grolier Club and Pierpont Morgan Library, 1988), p. xi.

19. On the textual history of Mill's *Autobiography* see *Autobiography and Literary Essays,* ed. John M. Robson and Jack Stillinger, in *Collected Works of John Stuart Mill,* vol. 1 (Toronto: University of Toronto Press, 1981), and Stillinger, "Who Wrote J. S. Mill's *Autobiography?*" *Victorian Studies* 27 (1983): 7–23.

20. For a discussion of the individual characteristics and the textual

authority of the three manuscripts see Jack Stillinger, "The Text of John Stuart Mill's *Autobiography*," *Bulletin of the John Rylands Library* 43 (September 1960): 220–42.

21. The publicity with which research materials once entered what has become the Harry Ransom Humanities Research Center at the University of Texas at Austin has been matched by the efforts the center has made recently to attract scholars to travel to Austin to consult those documents.

22. Arthur Freeman, while confirming my recollections of his own early experience, added the information about Boston University's successes in a letter dated 19 March 1991 (cited by permission). We can imagine how different our understanding of the Romantics would be if the Bodleian Library or the Cambridge University Library had invited Wordsworth, Coleridge, Byron, Shelley, and (by some wild fluke) Blake and Keats to donate their earliest poetic manuscripts.

23. Bruce, *The Nun of Lebanon* (London: Collins, 1951), p. 19.

24. Countess Guiccioli to Lord Byron, 16 September 1820.

25. The friend was Vera Cacciatore, then curator of the Keats-Shelley Memorial, Rome.

CHAPTER THREE
PRIVATE, CONFIDENTIAL, AND
PUBLIC MANUSCRIPTS

1. The first full account of Mary Jane ("Claire") Clairmont's pursuit of Byron, writing to him under the pseudonym "E. Trefusis," appeared in *"To Lord Byron": Feminine Profiles Based upon Unpublished Letters, 1807–1824* by "George Paston" (i.e., Emily Morse Symonds) and Peter Quennell (London: John Murray, 1939), pp. 202ff. See also, Leslie A. Marchand, *Byron: A Biography*, 3 vols. (New York: Alfred A. Knopf, 1957), 2:591–94 and passim.

2. On 23 August 1819, Byron's most unqualified declaration of love to Teresa Guiccioli was written in her copy of *Corinna* (an Italian translation of Guiccioli's favorite novel), in English, a language that she could not read at the time. For the full text see Iris Origo, *The Last Attachment: The Story of Byron and Teresa Guiccioli as Told in Their Unpublished Letters and Other Family Papers* (London: John Murray & Jonathan Cape; New York: Charles Scribner's Sons, 1949), pp. 112–13; or *Byron's Letters and Journals*, ed. Leslie A. Marchand, 12 vols. (London: John Murray, 1973–81), 6:215–16. I

explore implications of Byron's ambivalent message in *Shelley and his Circle*, vol. 7 (Cambridge: Harvard University Press, 1986), pp. 57–61.

3. See Lamb's Elia essay "The Two Races of Men," in *The Works of Charles and Mary Lamb*, ed. E. V. Lucas, 6 vols. (New York: Macmillan, 1913), 2:26–31.

4. See *Scott's Last Expedition: The Personal Journals of Captain R. F. Scott, CVO, RN, on His Journey to the South Pole*, with an introduction by Sir Vivian Fuchs (London: Folio Society, 1964).

5. Individual references in Godwin's journals are explicated and analyzed in William St. Clair, *The Godwins and the Shelleys*, and in the eight volumes to date of *Shelley and his Circle*, ed. Kenneth Neill Cameron (vols. 1–4) and Donald H. Reiman (vols. 5–8) (Cambridge: Harvard University Press, 1961–), where they can be traced by means of the indexes in vols. 2, 4, 6, and 8.

6. *The Diary of Joseph Farington*, ed. Kenneth Garlick, Angus Macintyre, and Kathryn Cave, 16 vols. (New Haven: Yale University Press for the Paul Mellon Centre for Studies in British Art, 1978–84); *The Diary of Benjamin Robert Haydon*, ed. Willard Bissell Pope, 5 vols. (Cambridge: Harvard University Press, 1960–63).

7. Though Robinson's expansive diary, in Dr. Williams's Library, London, has never been published in full, at least three extensive selections from it have appeared: *Diary, Reminiscences, and Correspondence of Henry Crabb Robinson*, ed. Thomas Sadler, 3 vols. (London: Macmillan & Co., 1869), contains substantial selections from Robinson's personal life and legal career, including comments on important trials he attended; *Henry Crabb Robinson on Books and Their Writers*, ed. Edith J. Morley (also Robinson's biographer), 3 vols. (London: J. M. Dent & Sons, 1938), also draws on his letters and his "Reminiscences," a document prepared for the public, which is sometimes quoted after the relevant passage from his diary (see, e.g., 1:234–36 and 389–90); and *The London Theatre, 1811–1866: Selections from the Diary of Henry Crabb Robinson*, ed. Eluned Brown (London: Society for Theatre Research, 1966).

8. *Anne Frank: The Diary of a Young Girl*, trans. B. M. Mooyaart-Doubleday, with an introduction by Eleanor Roosevelt and a new preface by George Stevens (New York: Pocket Books, 1953), p. [11], containing a facsimile of the manuscript inscription.

9. "Anne Frank n'en était pas encore à l'âge où, écrivant un journal, un adulte (surtout s'il est homme de lettres) pose devant la glace et pense à la postérité. Elle s'en fichait bien, de la postérité!" (*Journal*

de Anne Frank [Het Achterhuis], trans. T. Caren and Suzanne Lombard, preface by Daniel-Rops [Paris: Calmann-Lévy, 1950], p. ix).

10. *Anne Frank: The Critical Edition* (New York: Doubleday, 1989) was prepared by the Netherlands State Institute for War Documentation, edited by David Barnouw and Gerrold van der Stroom, and translated by Arnold J. Pomerans.

11. These letters were sold at Christie's, New York, on 8 December 1989.

12. In a postscript to Shelley's letter to Peacock from Bologna dated 9 November 1818, Mary Shelley wrote: "Keep Shelley's letters for I have no copies of them and I want to copy them when I return to England" (Shelley, *Letters*, 2:54). She actually made copies of many of Shelley's "Letters from Italy" as early as the 1820s, editing out some of the personal material, and then recopied and edited them slightly differently when she sent them to press in 1840 as part of her edition of Shelley's *Essays, Letters from Abroad, Translations, and Fragments* (see *Shelley and his Circle*, vol. 6, p. 678 and n. 10).

13. Moore's comment about Murray appears in the new edition of *The Journal of Thomas Moore*, ed. Wilfred S. Dowden, vol. 1 (Newark: University of Delaware Press, 1983), p. 187. Moore (or one of his heirs) destroyed almost all of Byron's letters to him after Moore had quoted substantial portions of them, with asterisks to indicate editorial deletions, in his two-volume *Letters and Journals of Lord Byron, with Notices of His Life* (London: John Murray, 1830–31). In "The Temptations of a Biographer: Thomas Moore and Byron" (*Byron Journal* 17 [1989]: 50–56), William St. Clair discusses the single letter (of at least 158) from Byron to Moore that is known to survive.

14. Natalie Zemon Davis, *Fiction in the Archives* (Stanford, Calif.: Stanford University Press, 1987).

15. Joseph Conrad, "Outside Literature," in *British and American Essays, 1905–1956*, ed. Carl L. Anderson and George Walton Williams (New York: Henry Holt & Co., 1959), p. 12, reprinted from Conrad, *Last Essays of Joseph Conrad*, intro. Richard Curle (Garden City, N.Y.: Doubleday, 1926), pp. 39–43.

16. *The Letters of Oscar Wilde*, ed. Rupert Hart-Davis (New York: Harcourt, Brace & World, 1962), pp. 253–54.

17. On the relations between Wilde and Whistler see Richard Ellmann, *Oscar Wilde* (New York: Vintage Books, 1988), pp. 131–34.

18. John A. Walker, one of a group of scholars editing Zola's

letters, reports that when he came to a manuscript addressed to Raoul Vast and Georges Ricourd that turned out to be Zola's commendatory letter prefatory to a novel by Vast and Ricourd, it "did not *look* like the manuscript of a letter, but like that of a text written for publication" (see "Editing Zola's Correspondence: When Is a Letter Not a Letter?" in *Editing Correspondence: Papers Given at the Fourteenth Annual Conference on Editorial Problems, University of Toronto . . . 1978* [New York: Garland Publishing, 1979], pp. 93–116).

19. For the text of this letter see *The Complete Works of Percy Bysshe Shelley* (Julian Edition), ed. Roger Ingpen and Walter E. Peck, vol. 10 (London: Ernest Benn; New York: Charles Scribner's Sons, 1926), pp. 417–18; and Shelley, *Letters*, 1:558–59. The error was first corrected in *Shelley and his Circle*, vol. 5, ed. Reiman (1973), p. 144, n. 9.

20. I first raised this issue as part of a commentary on John Keats's letter to his brothers of 5 January 1818 (*Shelley and his Circle*, 5:436–37).

21. On the effects of this early—and much later—patronage on Hunt's character and both his strengths and weaknesses as a man of letters see Donald H. Reiman, "Leigh Hunt in Literary History," in *The Life and Times of Leigh Hunt: Papers Delivered at a Symposium at the University of Iowa, April 13, 1984, Commemorating the 200th Anniversary of Leigh Hunt's Birth*, ed. Robert A. McCown (Iowa City: Friends of the University of Iowa Libraries, 1985), pp. 73–99, esp. pp. 76–77.

22. See the expanded and corrected text of Shelley's letter to Peacock of 17 July 1816 in *Shelley and his Circle*, vol. 7 (1986), p. 28, and the commentary on pp. 45–49.

23. During most of late 1815 and 1816 through the time Shelley spent on the Continent, although he used at intervals three intaglio seals to seal his letters with wax, he usually employed the more practical, up-to-date bourgeois wafer seals—red, orange, green, gray, or black (most of the exceptions being letters to creditors or to those from whom he wished to borrow money). As the bibliographical descriptions in *Shelley and his Circle* show, beginning with his letter to Byron of 8 September 1816, immediately after returning to England following his sojourn with Byron in Switzerland, Shelley usually sealed his letters to Byron through 1821 with wax, using the seal impression of a classical scene, the Judgment of Paris.

Shelley's apparent self-consciousness in this regard may have been part of a wider social phenomenon. Not only did members of his circle—Peacock, Hogg, and others—begin to seal their letters with wax more frequently about mid-1817, but in the chapter "Old Letters" in Gaskell's *Cranford* we find this remark: "The letters of Mrs. Jenkyns and her mother were fastened with a great round red wafer; for it was before Miss Edgeworth's *Patronage* [1814] had banished wafers from polite society" (p. 87).

24. Godwin shows his remarkable artfulness as a correspondent in all his letters dealing with money, but an epitomizing example is his letter to Shelley of 8 June 1818, the first he wrote to Shelley in Italy. In the text of this letter as sent to Shelley, Godwin crossed out (though leaving legible) some negative comments about Shelley's last letter (not extant); a copy of the letter that Godwin retained contains the same parts of the identical paragraph crossed out in the same (apparently) calculated way. The two manuscripts now rest side by side in the Abinger Collection (*Shelley and his Circle*, 6:654–55). The artfulness of Peacock and Sidney Smith also manifests itself most when they were dealing with patrons or others of higher social class. Hazlitt and Keats tried stubbornly to maintain their independence from such patronage. Keats was artful chiefly in his respect for the egos and prejudices of his friends; and both Hazlitt and Keats (occasionally) had to be artful when dealing with their publishers.

25. Ibid., 5:436–37.

26. *Letters from Lambeth: The Correspondence of the Reynolds Family with John Freeman Milward Dovaston, 1808–1815*, ed. Joanna Richardson (London: Boydell Press for the Royal Society of Literature, 1981), pp. 94, 187n; *The Letters of Charles and Mary Anne Lamb*, ed. Edwin W. Marrs, Jr., 3 vols. to date (Ithaca, N.Y.: Cornell University Press, 1975–), 2:22, 28 and n. 40, and passim.

27. *Shelley and his Circle*, 7:163–214.

28. Ibid., 7:300.

29. *Byron's Letters and Journals*, 6:14.

30. The eight short notes, numbered SC 595–602, appear in *Shelley and his Circle*, 7.298–304; for Dr. Fischer's commentary on them see 7:185–90.

31. The latest edition of this correspondence as a separate entity is *The Letters of Robert Browning and Elizabeth Barrett Barrett, 1845–1846*, ed. Elvan Kintner, 2 vols. (Cambridge: Harvard University Press, 1969).

32. For a reading text of these poems, with full annotation, see Kenneth Neill Cameron's edition of Shelley, *The Esdaile Notebook: A Volume of Early Poems* (New York: Alfred A. Knopf, 1964; cor-

rected repr., London: Faber & Faber, 1964). For Cameron's last thoughts on the text and annotation of the poems, see *Shelley and his Circle*, 4:911–1062. A facsimile edition, correcting some points in Cameron's work, is *The Esdaile Notebook: A Facsimile of the Holograph Copybook in The Carl H. Pforzheimer Library*, ed. Donald H. Reiman, *Manuscripts of the Younger Romantics*, vol. 1, *Percy Bysshe Shelley* (New York: Garland Publishing, 1985).

33. John Freeman, "Shelley's Letters to His Father," *Keats-Shelley Memorial Bulletin* 34 (1983): 1–15.

34. See Paul de Man, "Shelley Disfigured," and J. Hillis Miller, "The Critic as Host," in *Deconstruction and Criticism* (New York: Seabury Press, 1979), pp. 39–73 and 217–53, respectively.

35. See Donald H. Reiman, *Shelley's "The Triumph of Life": A Critical Study, Based on a Text Newly Edited from the Bodleian Manuscript* (Urbana: University of Illinois Press, 1965); idem, *Percy Bysshe Shelley* (New York: Twayne Publishers, 1969; Updated Edition, Boston: Twayne and G. K. Hall, 1990), and idem, "Shelley's 'The Triumph of Life': The Biographical Problem," *PMLA* 78 (December 1963): 536–50, reprinted in Reiman, *Romantic Texts and Contexts* (Columbia: University of Missouri Press, 1987), pp. 289–320. The latter essay was the first to deal in detail with Shelley's use of Rousseau and Rousseau's *Julie; ou, La Nouvelle Héloïse* in "The Triumph."

36. See *Prometheus Unbound*, 4.236–68, and the annotation in *Shelley's Poetry and Prose*, ed. Donald H. Reiman and Sharon B. Powers (New York: W. W. Norton, 1977), pp. 201–2.

37. Though the manuscript was available for de Man's scrutiny throughout the period between the late 1960s, when he first began to give lectures on "The Triumph of Life," and 1979, when he published *Deconstruction and Criticism*, there is no evidence that he examined the primary evidence himself, depending entirely upon the selection of canceled readings from the manuscript given in my *Shelley's "The Triumph of Life": A Critical Study*. Scholars now can consult the facsimile of the manuscript, edited with a virtually complete transcription and textual notes, in *Peter Bell the Third . . . (Bodleian MS. Shelley adds. c.5, folios 50–69 and "The Triumph of Life" . . . (Bodleian MS. Shelley adds. c.4, folios 18–58)*, ed. Donald H. Reiman, *The Bodleian Shelley Manuscripts*, vol. 1 (New York: Garland Publishing, 1986).

38. In my discussion of the manuscript for the facsimile edition (see n. 37), I have shown that Mary Shelley's comments on the poem

make clear that she knew nothing about "The Triumph of Life" until after Shelley's death. If Shelley had told Edward Williams anything relevant about it, Williams carried the secret to his grave when he drowned with Shelley.

CHAPTER FOUR

PRIVATE AND PUBLIC MANUSCRIPTS:
AUTHORIAL INTENTION AND READER RESPONSE

1. Once editors or commentators on a manuscript have established and labeled it within its original functional category as a *public, confidential,* or *private* document, the next step in analysis may be to comment on any distortion of its implications that may arise because it is a *private* manuscript now made *public.*

2. Pierre Lévêque, *The Greek Adventure,* trans. Miriam Kochan (Cleveland: World Publishing, 1968), pp. 54–55.

3. SC 656, edited by William St. Clair, in *Shelley and his Circle,* 8:619–95. St. Clair's essay "Trelawny's Lost Years" and his commentary on details of the manuscript occupy pp. 611–18 and 695–704, respectively.

4. William St. Clair, *Trelawny: The Incurable Romancer* (New York: Vanguard Press, 1977) was reviewed by Donald H. Reiman—along with St. Clair's edition of *Adventures of a Younger Son* and another biography of Trelawny—in "Trelawny and the Decay of Lying," *Review* 1 (1979): 275–94.

5. The published edition is *Maria Gisborne & Edward E. Williams, Shelley's Friends: Their Journals and Letters,* ed. Frederick L. Jones (Norman: University of Oklahoma Press, 1951). As George H. Ford pointed out in a review in *Modern Philology* 50 (August 1952): 69–72, Jones's edition was done from "microfilm or some other form of copy," resulting in numerous errors and omissions that he could have avoided by consulting the original. With the benefit of Ford's extensive list of errata, the edition serves our purpose for illustration of a type of journal. Mary Shelley's relevant letters are those to Maria Gisborne of 8 May, 18 June, and 7 July 1820 (see *The Letters of Mary Wollstonecraft Shelley,* ed. Betty T. Bennett, 3 vols. [Baltimore: Johns Hopkins University Press, 1980–88], 1:145–49, 152–54).

6. See *Maria Gisborne & Edward E. Williams, Shelley's Friends,* pp. 35–36 (with one correction from George H. Ford's review).

7. *Shelley and his Circle,* 6:817.

8. Ibid., 6:831.

9. John Freeman, "Shelley's Letters to His Father," *Keats-Shelley Memorial Bulletin* 34 (1983): 1–15.

10. The existence of this cache of manuscripts was first called to my attention by a very helpful woman at the Fitzwilliam Museum Library in Cambridge; the manuscripts were subsequently tracked from London to New York. The fullest public accounts of the Guiccioli-Gamba papers now in the Carl H. Pforzheimer Shelley and His Circle Collection, the New York Public Library, appear in volumes 7 and 8 of *Shelley and his Circle,* especially in Doucet Devin Fischer's essays " 'Countesses and Cobblers' Wives': Byron's Venetian Mistresses" and "Countess Guiccioli's Byron" (7:163–214 and 373–487, respectively).

11. This passage, edited from my commentary on the Pforzheimer manuscript accessioned as TG 131, will appear in volume 9 of *Shelley and his Circle;* it is included here with the kind permission of the Carl and Lily Pforzheimer Foundation, Inc., which holds the copyright.

12. Since the case of Salinger's letters restricted the right of the use of unpublished materials against the wishes of the writer or the writer's heirs (and a similar case involving the papers of L. Ron Hubbard, the founder of Scientology, resulted in a comparable decision in favor of the writer's estate), the Congress of the United States has moved to rewrite the copyright laws to allow quotation and citation of unpublished material for scholarly purposes, while still protecting the financial rights of writers and their heirs.

13. *Selected Letters of James Joyce,* ed. Richard Ellmann (New York: Viking Press, 1975), p. vii.

14. The first eleven of Hazlitt's confessional letters to be published appeared in 1894 as part of a factual supplement to a private printing of *Liber Amoris,* limited to five hundred copies, with an introduction by Richard Le Gallienne, set in the context of the development of the creative work that grew out of them.

15. Charles Rossman, "The New 'Ulysses': The Hidden Controversy," *New York Review of Books,* 8 December 1988, pp. 53–58.

16. As Jon Stallworthy wrote to me in 1989 on this issue, one cannot have "a better guide through the minefield of a dead author's papers than a good literary executor" who has "no financial interest in what to publish and when," one who is "committed to promoting an informed interest in the author's work and generating thereby royalties for the author's heirs" but "*not* at the expense of the author's

reputation or the peace of mind of his surviving family and friends" (quoted by permission).

17. On this issue see Donald H. Reiman, *Romantic Texts and Contexts,* p. 201n.

18. *Shelley and his Circle,* 2:762; Thomas Jefferson Hogg, *Life of Percy Bysshe Shelley,* vol. 1 (London: Edward Moxon, 1858), p. 358.

19. See *Shelley and his Circle,* 6:672–80, esp. 678 n. 10.

20. See Richard D. Altick, "Harold Skimpole Revisited," in McCown, *Life and Times of Leigh Hunt,* pp. 1–15.

21. See *The Correspondence of Stephen Crane,* ed. Stanley Wertheim and Paul Sorrentino, 2 vols. (New York: Columbia University Press, 1988). For evaluations of the charges against Beer see reviews by Harold Beaver in *TLS,* 20–26 January 1989, pp. 55–56 (Wertheim's reply in a letter to the editor is in ibid., 3–9 March 1989) and by Stanton Garner in *Documentary Editing* 11 (June 1989): 51–55.

22. The full text of Shelley's letter to Peacock describing his trip with Byron around Lake Geneva was first published, with commentary, in *Shelley and his Circle,* 7:25–49. In "Documenting Revision: Shelley's Lake Geneva Diary and the Dialogue with Byron in *History of a Six Weeks' Tour,*" *Keats-Shelley Journal* 39 (1990): 66–82, Robert Brinkley, referring to a partial draft of a diary that Shelley kept during the period in Bodleian MS. Shelley adds. e. 16, corrected my inferences about the relationship of the text of this letter to the published work.

23. Frederick L. Jones's *Mary Shelley's Journal* (Norman: University of Oklahoma Press, 1947), has been superseded by *The Journals of Mary Shelley: 1814–1844,* ed. Paula A. Feldman and Diana Scott-Kilvert, 2 vols. (Oxford: Clarendon Press, 1987). Jones's *Maria Gisborne & Edward E. Williams, Shelley's Friends* was reviewed by George H. Ford in *Modern Philology* 50 (August 1952): 69–72.

24. For the record, the note to Murray in *Byron's Letters and Journals,* vol. 7 (1977), p. 162, beginning "The Italian vespers" is written on the other side of the sheet on which the corrections for *Marino Faliero* dated 28 August 1820 appear (7:164–65). Likewise, the note to Murray beginning "The 'Advice to Julia' is excellent" (7:165) actually belongs with the further corrections to *Marino Faliero* dated 31 August 1820 (7:169–70).

25. I am grateful to Leslie A. Marchand for sharing this discovery with me and for granting me permission to cite it here.

26. *Byron's Letters and Journals,* 8:119.

27. The owner of the manuscript who had deposited the letter at the Pierpont Morgan Library eventually withdrew it and resold it at auction. I have checked the facts of the case once more against a facsimile of the entire letter that appeared when it was offered for sale again, in the spring of 1991, in Catalogue 22 of Lion Heart Autographs, Inc., of New York. Unpublished portions of the letter are quoted by permission of John Murray, Ltd., owner of the copyright.

28. See Giles Barber's "Galignani's and the Publication of English Books in France from 1800 to 1852," *The Library,* Fifth Series, 14 (December 1961), pp. 267–86, as well as the other sources noted in *Shelley and his Circle,* 8:1014 n. 13.

CHAPTER FIVE

MODERN MANUSCRIPTS AND THE PUBLISHED TEXT

1. Jean-Louis Lebrave, "Rough Drafts: A Challenge to Uniformity in Editing," *TEXT* 3 (1987): 135–42.

2. The *Bodleian Shelley Manuscripts,* general editor Donald H. Reiman, comprises fourteen volumes to date (New York: Garland Publishing, 1986–); *The Manuscripts of the Younger Romantics,* Donald H. Reiman, general editor and area editor for Shelley and Byron, with Jerome J. McGann, area editor for Byron, and Jack Stillinger, area editor for Keats, numbers nineteen volumes to date (New York: Garland Publishing, 1985–).

3. Mary A. Quinn, ed., *The Mask of Anarchy Draft Notebook: A Facsimile of Huntington MS. HM 2177,* in *The Manuscripts of the Younger Romantics,* vol. 4, *Percy Bysshe Shelley* (1990).

4. Among the many statements of the position that an author's press-copy manuscript, if extant, normally is preferred as copy-text over the printed edition that was based on it are several in Fredson T. Bowers, *Essays in Bibliography, Text, and Editing* (Charlottesville: University Press of Virginia, 1975), especially in "Practical Texts and Definitive Editions" (pp. 412–39) and "Remarks on Eclectic Texts" (pp. 488–528). Bowers's view has been defended, rationalized, and codified by G. Thomas Tanselle in his *Selected Studies in Bibliography* (Charlottesville: University Press of Virginia, 1979), especially in "Greg's Theory of Copy-Text and the Editing of American Literature" (pp. 245–307) and "The Editorial Problem of Final Authorial

Intention" (pp. 309–53), as well as in the three essays in Tanselle's *Textual Criticism since Greg, a Chronicle: 1950–1985* (Charlottes-ville: University Press of Virginia, 1987)—the first of which is the same "Greg's Theory of Copy-Text and the Editing of American Literature"—which taken together represent a comprehensive his-torical appraisal of recent writings on editorial theory from the per-spective of the Greg-Bowers-Tanselle tradition.

5. Jane Austen, *Volume the First,* ed. R. W. Chapman, The Jane Library (New York: Schocken Books, 1985), p. xix.

6. Facsimiles of these fair copies are not now readily available, but a volume of Shelley's fair-copy holographs, including the "Trelawny manuscripts" and those mentioned in the following note, will appear in a volume in *The Manuscripts of the Younger Romantics.*

7. The fair-copy holograph manuscript of *Julian and Maddalo* is in the Pierpont Morgan Library, and that of "Athanase: A Fragment" is in the Pforzheimer Collection (transcribed as SC 582, with facsim-iles of four of its tiny pages in *Shelley and his Circle,* 7:132–39). One of the lyrics to Sophia Stacey, written by Shelley in a postscript to Mary Shelley's letter of March 1820 (now in the Bibliotheque Bodmeriana, near Geneva, Switzerland), was reproduced in facsimile in Margaret Crum's catalog *English and American Autographs in the Bodmeriana* (Cologny-Genève: Fondation Martin Bodmer, 1977), p. [61].

8. For the copy-text manuscript of *Beppo,* edited by Jerome J. McGann, see *Shelley and his Circle,* 7:258–98; the manuscript of *Marino Faliero,* edited by Thomas L. Ashton, will appear as the first item in vol. 9.

9. Examples of these small slips in facsimile include Shelley's holo-graph of "Athanase: A Fragment" (see n. 7) and Mary Shelley's transcription of *Peter Bell the Third,* reproduced in full in volume 1 of *The Bodleian Shelley Manuscripts.* Mary Shelley also prepared the press copy of *The Mask of Anarchy* now in the Library of Congress (see vol. 2 [1985] of *The Manuscripts of the Younger Romantics*) and probably the lost press copy for *Prometheus Unbound* and many, if not all, of its accompanying poems (see Neil Fraistat's introduction to vol. 9 [1991] of *The Bodleian Shelley Manuscripts*). In *Shelley and his Circle,* vol. 9 (forthcoming), I argue that Claire Clairmont probably copied Shelley's *Oedipus Tyrannus; or, Swellfoot the Ty-rant* for the press. I do not know whether Clairmont or Mary Shelley prepared the press copy of *The Cenci,* which was printed in Italy under Shelley's supervision.

10. Pforzheimer Collection, Huntana 55. This note was given to

a sale for the benefit of the Keats-Shelley Memorial Association by Colonel Trevor Leigh-Hunt and acquired by the Carl H. Pforzheimer Library in 1955.

11. See Donald H. Reiman, "Leigh Hunt in Literary History," in McCown, *The Life and Times of Leigh Hunt*, pp. 73–99.

12. As Peter L. Shillingsburg pointed out to me, Thackeray (like Edward Lear and other writers of the period) often illustrated his personal letters. For examples see the facsimiles tipped in as frontispieces to volumes of *The Letters and Private Papers of William Makepiece Thackeray*, ed. Gordon N. Ray, 4 vols. (Cambridge: Harvard University Press, 1945–46).

13. Some publications in the year 1991 mark a further weakening in the respect for privacy of others—a deterioration that has been accelerating in recent years. With the consent of her heirs, the tapes poet Anne Sexton made for her psychotherapist, revealing her private weaknesses, were heard and used by Diane Wood Middlebrook in *Anne Sexton: A Biography* (Boston: Houghton Mifflin, 1991). Also published posthumously, *The Journals of John Cheever*, ed. Benjamin Cheever and Robert Gottleib (New York: Alfred A. Knopf, 1991), includes about a twentieth of the raw private journals of the novelist. In the published selections, Cheever describes his family quarrels and his homosexual encounters.

The arguments advanced by those responsible for making public these private materials were that Sexton was a confessional poet who made her personal pain the staple of her art and that Cheever wanted his unhappiness known not only to his family but to the world. Excerpts from the diaries of Sappho Durrell suggesting that her father, Lawrence Durrell, carried on an incestuous relationship with her also appeared in 1991, in the October issue of *Granta*, after Sappho's mother Eve Durrell sought an injunction to prevent the publication. In this case, there was a more cogent and obvious justification for publication, because Sappho Durrell, whose writing was at issue, had asked a friend to publish her diaries after she and her father were dead so that, in simple justice, the world might know what lay behind her mental illness and her suicide in 1985 at age thirty-three. In each case, the publisher—and in the first two cases the heirs—stood to gain something from the salacious nature of the revelations. And in the first two cases, the occasion and manner of these publications may not have been tactful enough to allay the distrust of others whose diaries and private papers, if left undestroyed, might someday prove to be more valuable to society.

14. For Mary Shelley's efforts in the late 1830s to provide readers

with an acceptable text of Shelley's writings see Bennett's *The Letters of Mary Wollstonecraft Shelley,* 2:298–347.

15. See George Edward Woodberry's notes on "To the Queen of My Heart" under "Doubtful Poems" in his Centenary Edition of *The Complete Poetical Works of Percy Bysshe Shelley,* 4 vols. (Boston: Houghton Mifflin, 1892), 4:390–92. According to an article in the *Eclectic Review* (1851), the man who wrote the poem and published it as Shelley's to prove a point was James Augustus St. John (1801–75 [*DNB*]).

16. See Nicholas A. Joukovsky, "Peacock before *Headlong Hall:* A New Look at His Early Years," *Keats-Shelley Memorial Bulletin* 36 (1985): 1–40; on Hogg's malicious suggestions see pp. 31–32.

17. "Memoirs of Percy Bysshe Shelley," quoted from *The Works of Thomas Love Peacock,* ed. H. F. B. Brett-Smith and C. E. Jones, Halliford Edition, vol. 8 (London: Constable & Co.; New York: Gabriel Wells, 1924–34), p. 40.

18. The facts on this point are fully and clearly delineated by Jane Millgate in the first chapter of *Scott's Last Edition: A Study in Publishing History* (Edinburgh: Edinburgh University Press, 1987).

19. See Ernest J. Simmons, *Tolstoy* (London: Routledge & Kegan Paul, 1973), p. 178; a copy of this translation, with its textual importance described, appeared in the William Reese Company's literature catalog number 71 (New Haven, Conn., 1989), item 1229.

20. On the important distinction between individual "texts" and the ideal "work" see G. Thomas Tanselle, *A Rationale of Textual Criticism* (Philadelphia: University of Pennsylvania Press, 1989).

21. Hershel Parker, *Flawed Texts and Verbal Icons: Literary Authority in American Fiction* (Evanston, Ill.: Northwestern University Press, 1984).

22. My views, which are indebted to D. W. Gotshalk's system of aesthetics in *Art and the Social Order* (Chicago: University of Chicago Press, 1947), have only been sketched in the introduction and afterword to *Romantic Texts and Contexts* (1987); a more imaginative articulation of them follows in chapter 6.

23. Central publications on this subject by these three scholar-critics include Jerome J. McGann's *Critique of Modern Textual Criticism* (Chicago: University of Chicago Press, 1983); D. F. McKenzie's *Bibliography and the Sociology of Texts: The Panizzi Lectures, 1985* (London: British Library, 1986); and Jack Stillinger's *Multiple Authorship and the Myth of Solitary Genius* (New York: Oxford University Press, 1991).

24. For accounts of some classic textual and bibliographical errors

see Bruce Harkness, "Bibliography and the Novelistic Fallacy," *Studies in Bibliography* 12 (1959): 59–73, reprinted in *Bibliography and Textual Criticism: English and American Literature, 1700 to the Present,* ed. O. M. Brack, Jr., and Warner Barnes (Chicago: University of Chicago Press, 1969), pp. 23–40.

25. See Reiman, *Romantic Texts and Contexts,* pp. 167–80.

26. One aspect of the expectations of early nineteenth-century authors regarding the authority their press-copy manuscripts that deserves further exploration is the frequency with which printers and bookseller-publishers retained these manuscripts after the printing and publishing process was completed. There is evidence in the exchanges between Byron and John Murray and between Mary Shelley and Charles Ollier that publishers regarded the manuscripts of works they published as their own personal property—at least the manuscripts of works they agreed to publish at their own expense (whether or not they purchased the copyrights).

27. Though the phrase "The Gutenberg Galaxy," as popularized by Marshall McLuhan's 1962 book of that title, fell out of favor when the enthusiastic fad response to McLuhan's ideas receded, some of the central conceptions he popularized are even more significant now, at the dawn of the age of random or nonsequential retrieval of information, than they were when he first helped bring them to the attention of the public. Those of us involved in the theoretical issues of textual studies (as pursued in recent years in the Society for Textual Scholarship) now recognize that the Gutenberg era's use of printing by forms (and its apparently nonsequential arrangement of pages on the press before folding and gathering) was a major milestone in a continuing movement from the purely sequential scroll book, to the codex manuscript (in which the reader could flip quickly back and forth to compare passages), to the random-access memories now gaining ascendance in the era of electronic information.

28. See *Johnson on Shakespeare,* ed. Arthur Sherbo, vol. 7 of *The Yale Edition of the Works of Samuel Johnson* (New Haven: Yale University Press, 1968), p. 107.

29. I summarized some of the arguments of Johnson's editors and contrasted Johnson's attitude with that of Cowper in a talk given at the 1985 Toronto Conference on Editorial Problems and published as "Gentlemen Authors and Professional Writers: Notes on the History of Editing Texts of the 18th and 19th Centuries," in *Editing and Editors: A Retrospect,* ed. Richard Landon (New York: AMS Press, 1988), pp. 99–136.

30. Stillinger's seven volumes in *The Manuscripts of the Younger*

Romantics (1985–88) were supplemented by his edition of *John Keats, Poetry Manuscripts at Harvard: A Facsimile Edition* (Cambridge: Harvard University Press, 1990).

31. Stillinger (who discusses the contributions of Keats's friends and editors to his poems in more detail in *Multiple Authorship and the Myth of Solitary Genius,* pp. 25–49) chose the *Lamia* volume of 1820 as copy-text for his edition of *The Poems of John Keats* (Cambridge: Harvard University Press, 1978).

32. See Harry Buxton Forman, *The Shelley Library: An Essay in Bibliography* (London: Reeves & Turner for the Shelley Society, 1886), pp. 71–87; *Shelley and his Circle,* 5:141–89; and Tatsuo Tokoo, ed., *Bodleian MS. Shelley d. 3: A Facsimile Edition with Full Transcription and Textual Notes,* vol. 8 (1988) of *The Bodleian Shelley Manuscripts,* pp. xi–xxi.

33. Other volumes featuring long stanzaic poems that either were or pretended to be such escapist romances include *Richard the First,* by Sir James Bland Burges (1801; Spenserian stanzas); *Gertrude of Wyoming,* by Thomas Campbell (1809; Spenserian); *The Four Slaves of Cythera,* by Robert Bland (1809; within a poem in couplets Bland introduces a 68-stanza poem in what is referred to in a note as "the octave stanza, and the manner of the Italian school"); *Sir Edgar; A Tale in Two Cantos,* by Francis Hodgson (1810; eight-line stanza ending in an Alexandrine); *Psyche,* by Mary Tighe (1811; Spenserian); *Hermilda in Palestine,* by Edward, Lord Thurlow (1812; ottava rima); and *Orlando in Roncesvalles,* by John Herman Merivale (1814; ottava rima). All of the men named were friends or acquaintances of Byron's.

34. For example, in the texts of both *Childe Harold's Pilgrimage* and *Don Juan* in volumes 2 and 5 of *Lord Byron: The Complete Poetical Works* (Oxford: Clarendon Press, 1980 and 1986), McGann substituted arabic numerals, found in Byron's manuscripts, for the roman numerals that head the stanzas of these poems in the printed editions of Byron's poems. Not only does this change violate McGann's later theory but it is contrary to the contemporary evidence of Byron's own intentions. As David V. Erdman points out in his facsimile edition of the various manuscripts of *Childe Harold's Pilgrimage,* in *The Manuscripts of the Younger Romantics,* vol. 6, *Lord Byron* (1991), Byron specifically wrote to Murray on 5 September 1811 about *Childe Harold:* "The Stanzas had better be numbered in Roman characters" (see *Byron's Letters and Journals,* vol. 2 [1973], p. 91).

35. A rather dramatic exception to this statement—one that by its strangeness actually helps to establish the general rule for which I have been arguing—appeared for sale in May 1991 as item 180, Occasional List 91, issued by Ximenes Rare Books, of New York. There César Moreau's *Rise and Progress of the Silk Trade in England* (London: Treuttel and Würtz, Treuttel, Jun. and Richter; Paris and Strasbourgh: Treuttel and Würtz, February 1826) is described as "a most unusual production, lithographed throughout from the author's manuscript. The text consists of a title-page (verso blank) and 18 closely-printed pages of elaborate statistical tables and accompanying historical commentary. Moreau (1791–1860) was a French Vice Consul in London. He published a number of interesting works of economic history, most of them in this remarkable format."

Because of the extreme rarity of this work and its method of production, its eighteen pages commanded a price of $2,250. Yet Moreau's persistence in employing this technique of production shows that it was technically feasible for all authors, after the development of lithography, to present their works to the world as Blake did—exactly as they had personally prepared them, without any unauthorized alterations by publisher or printer—had that consideration been paramount to them. And as we saw at the end of the last chapter, it would even have been possible for them, using lithography, to revise and make any necessary corrections in their work.

CHAPTER SIX

MODERN MANUSCRIPTS AND PERSONALIST POETICS

1. *The Poetical Works of Gerard Manley Hopkins,* ed. W. H. Gardner and N. H. MacKenzie, 4th ed. (London: Oxford University Press, 1967), p. 108.

2. Although I had planned to add an appendix to list further examples of this trope, my friends and I were able to accumulate so few in three years of searching that I have been able to cite most of these in the text and notes of this chapter.

3. See, e.g., Guido Cavalcanti's "Ballata dall'eslio" ("Perch' i'non spero di tornar giammai"), in which the poet addresses his "Ballatetta" as a person throughout, or the final lines of Lapo Gianni's *ballatas* beginning "Dolce è 'l pesier che mi notrica il core" and "Questa rosa novella."

4. Milton, *Areopagitica* (1644), fifth paragraph.

5. *Shelley's Poetry and Prose*, p. 388.

6. See Barry Menikoff, *Robert Louis Stevenson and "The Beach of Falesà": A Study in Victorian Publishing* (Stanford, Calif.: Stanford University Press, 1984).

7. See the editions of John Clare by Eric Robinson and his colleagues, e.g., *John Clare*, ed. Eric Robinson and David Powell, The Oxford Authors (Oxford: Oxford University Press, 1984), pp. xxi–xxii, xxx.

8. If one were tempted to carry the analogy forward to a Shandean degree, it could be said that if the original obstetrician at the time of delivery bobbed the child's nose by intention or through accident and if that child (unlike Tristram) grew to adulthood happy, well-adjusted, and well-liked with a short, neat nose instead of the large economy-size one with which he had been conceived, few with the person's welfare at heart would recommend another operation to restore the feature to its original proportions. Not only would the surgery inflict pain and suffering but the person's friends might be shocked both by his new appearance and by the values of one who had submitted to such a procedure merely to undo something that nobody except his parents and the attending physician knew had ever happened. Moreover, such an attempt to restore to an adult's face what he had lost as a child might well prove fruitless, since there could be no guarantee that the belated restoration would actually produce the same appearance that the face would have assumed had its original feature developed and aged naturally. On the other hand, if photos survived that show the appearance of the child before the transforming surgery or accident, there might be no harm — and likely some interest and value — in showing it to friends and physicians of the child. (Thus I justify under my metaphorical system the production of facsimiles and editions of prepublication versions of any literary work.)

9. See Forman, *The Shelley Library*, pp. 71–87.

10. See *Shelley and his Circle*, 5:141–89; and Tatsuo Tokoo, *Bodleian MS. Shelley d. 3*, pp. xi–xxi.

11. Forman, *The Shelley Library*, p. 75; from *Fraser's Magazine* (March 1862).

12. This annotated copy is now in the Harry Ransom Humanities Research Center, University of Texas at Austin. By February 1821 Shelley also found aesthetic flaws in the text; in a letter to Ollier, he asked whether "there is any expectation of a second edition of the

'Revolt of Islam'? I have many corrections to make in it, and one part will be wholly remodelled" (Shelley, *Letters*, 2:263).

13. See *Shelley and his Circle*, 6:926–27, 931–34.

14. See Forman, *The Shelley Library*, pp. 77–80; Frederick A. Pottle explored the question further in his Yale dissertation, published as *Shelley and Browning: A Myth and Some Facts*, foreword by William Lyon Phelps (Chicago: Pembroke Press, 1923).

15. Gary Taylor, "The Fortunes of Oldcastle," *Shakespeare Survey* 38 (1985): 85–100. In "William Shakespeare, Richard James, and the House of Cobham," *RES*, n.s. 38 (August 1987): 334–54, Taylor provides additional information about Dr. Richard James (1592–1638), the historian whose dedicatory epistle to Sir Henry Bourchier of ca. 1634 is the chief source of our information on the circumstances of the censorship of *Henry IV, Part 1*.

16. Or in scholarship on nineteenth-century figures. Taylor cites as "the most explicit deposition" on the change and the reasons for it the autograph letter from Dr. Richard James (see n. 15). Taylor argues convincingly in "William Shakespeare, Richard James, and the House of Cobham" that James, "a friend of Ben Jonson and librarian to Sir Robert Cotton," probably wrote this letter "c. 1634" (Taylor, "Fortunes of Oldcastle," p. 86). James could have no first-hand knowledge of Shakespeare's supposed troubles with the authorities in 1597, because he was five years old at the time. From the passages quoted, it is clear that James is a Puritan hostile to Shakespeare's treatment of the character, whether named for Sir John Oldcastle or Sir John "Falstaffe" or "Fastollf," who James declares was "a man not inferior [of] Vertue though not so famous in pietie as the other" and also a Lollard stalwart. Thus, even if James had access to the basic story of the censorship directly from the mouths of Shakespeare's contemporaries and friends, we cannot assume that he transmitted it reliably. Having a quarrel with Shakespeare's portrayal of Sir John, James (like Shelley's detractors John Taylor Coleridge and Robert Southey) was a person likely to retail—and embroider—any gossip about how Shakespeare was rebuked and disciplined for it.

Scholars of nineteenth-century literature have learned to discount all stories based on such hearsay by younger members of the Shelley circle (such as Thornton Hunt) or by those who never knew the poet (such as Jane, Lady Shelley) unless these stories can be corroborated by reliable contemporary documentary evidence. Renaissance scholars, with less evidence available to support (or disprove) their theories, like cosmologists, may be tempted to invent more than they can discover.

17. Though Taylor develops an elaborate scenario in "William Shakespeare, Richard James, and the House of Cobham" to prove that Shakespeare was still smarting from the censorship of the name Oldcastle by the time he wrote *Merry Wives,* this second argument weakens the case in "The Fortunes of Oldcastle." Taylor notes that by the spring of 1596/97—the date Taylor would prefer for the court performance of *The Merry Wives of Windsor,* "Sir William [Brooke] was dead; his son Henry, though now Lord Cobham, was not Lord Chamberlain, or a member of the Privy Council, or an old friend of any influential courtier. As [David] McKeen says [in " 'A Memory of Honour': A Study of the House of Cobham in Kent in the Reign of Elizabeth I" (Ph.D. thesis, University of Birmingham, 1966), pp. 997–98], 'The new lord was fighting for his political life' in March and April" ("William Shakespeare, Richard James, and the House of Cobham," p. 349). If, as Taylor argues, Shakespeare felt free to retaliate against the Brookes through his use of the name Brooke in *Merry Wives,* he certainly had ample opportunity to revive the name Oldcastle in his plays during the reign of James I, had he felt moved to do so. And if he had done so, the evidence would appear in the folio text of 1623.

18. See Reiman, *Romantic Texts and Contexts,* pp. 174–75.

19. Allen Ginsberg, *Howl: Original Draft Facsimile, Transcript and Variant Versions, Fully Annotated by Author, with Contemporaneous Correspondence, Account of First Public Reading, Legal Skirmishes, Precursor Texts and Bibliography,* ed. Barry Mills (New York: Harper & Row, 1986). I cite this below as *Howl Variorum.*

20. See appendix 4, "Model Texts: Inspirations Precursor to HOWL," *Howl Variorum,* pp. 175–88.

21. *The Complete Works of William Hazlitt,* ed. P. P. Howe, vol. 11 (London: J. M. Dent & Sons, 1932), p. 16.

22. D. C. Greetham, "Textual and Literary Theory: Redrawing the Matrix," *Studies in Bibliography* 42 (1989): 1–24.

23. Donald H. Reiman, "Research Revisited: Scholarship and the Fine Art of Teaching," *College English* 23 (October 1961): 10–12.

24. The contraction during the past fifty years of the readership for both good literature and criticism explains the so-called crisis in literary studies, which is not a crisis that was caused—or that can be ameliorated—by any person, but, rather, by a new condition of technological progress in our society that will never go away. On the

brighter side, this (re)shrinkage of the interest in "good" or "serious" literature enables students of earlier literary periods to appreciate better the situation faced by writers and critics before the mid-nineteenth century than was possible for students of literature from about 1860 to 1960.

25. T. S. Eliot, "Shelley and Keats," in *The Use of Poetry and the Use of Criticism: Studies in the Relation of Criticism to Poetry in England* (London: Faber & Faber, 1933), pp. 87–102.

26. C. S. Lewis in *English Romantic Poets: Modern Essays in Criticism,* ed. M. H. Abrams (New York: Oxford University Press, 1960), p. 259. The essay "Shelley, Dryden, and Mr. Eliot" was taken from Lewis's collection *Rehabilitations and Other Essays* (London: Oxford University Press, 1939).

27. Lewis, "Shelley, Dryden, and Mr. Eliot," pp. 262–63.

28. Frederick A. Pottle, "The Case of Shelley," *PMLA* 67 (1952): 589–608, revised by Pottle and reprinted in Abrams, *English Romantic Poets,* pp. 289–306. On the New Critics and their reasons for denigrating Shelley, see Alexander Karanikas, *Tillers of a Myth: Southern Agrarians as Social and Literary Critics* (Madison: University of Wisconsin Press, 1966).

29. Frederick A. Pottle, letter to author, 1 June 1980, quoted by permission of Christopher Pottle.

INDEX

❖

The subject of this book being the relevance of modern manuscripts to the humane and personal influences in modern life and scholarship, this index is organized around the names of people—chiefly the writers, collectors, readers, and students of manuscripts—ancient, medieval, and modern. The index treats abstract topics selectively and does not attempt to recapitulate the data in chapter and section headings.

INDEX